" GOOD REVIEWS "

A COMPREHENSIVE GUIDE TO ONLINE REVIEWS AND PLATFORMS

RAJ VARMA

RiVirtual Inc

NewDelhi • London

LUEROSE PUBLISHERS
India | U.K.

Copyright © CXO Inc 2024

All rights reserved by author. No part of this publication may be reproduced, stored in a retrieval system or transmitted in any form or by any means, electronic, mechanical, photocopying, recording or otherwise, without the prior permission of the author. Although every precaution has been taken to verify the accuracy of the information contained herein, the publisher assumes no responsibility for any errors or omissions. No liability is assumed for damages that may result from the use of information contained within.

BlueRose Publishers takes no responsibility for any damages, losses, or liabilities that may arise from the use or misuse of the information, products, or services provided in this publication.

For permissions requests or inquiries regarding this publication,
please contact:

BLUEROSE PUBLISHERS
www.BlueRoseONE.com
info@bluerosepublishers.com
+91 8882 898 898
+4407342408967

ISBN: 978-93-5989-478-2

Cover design: Shivam
Typesetting: Namrata Saini

First Edition: July 2024

Dedication

"To the past that shaped me, the present that nurtures me, and the future that awaits me."

Forward

In our increasingly digital world, online reviews have become an invaluable resource for consumers making important purchasing decisions. Whether searching for the best local restaurant, researching the latest consumer electronics, or vetting service providers, we have come to rely on the collective wisdom and experiences of others shared across a myriad of online platforms.

This comprehensive guide is a timely and essential read for anyone navigating the complex landscape of online reviews. The author provides an in-depth exploration of the major review platforms— from Google and Facebook to Yelp, TripAdvisor, and Amazon— outlining their unique features, their importance for businesses, and strategies for leveraging them effectively.

Beyond just understanding the review platforms, this book delves into the psychological reasons behind how online reviews influence consumer behavior and purchasing decisions. Insights into building trust, managing reputation, and responding to feedback empower readers to harness the power of online reviews for their own benefit— whether as a savvy consumer or a business—seeking to thrive in the digital age.

As our reliance on online information continues to grow, this book equips readers with the knowledge and tools needed to make informed choices, drive business success, and navigate the ever-evolving world of digital reputation. It is a must-read for anyone seeking to master the art of online reviews and leverage them for personal or professional gain.

Contents

Introduction 1

Chapter 1: The Power of Online Reviews 6
    The Significance of Online Reviews in the Modern
    Consumer Landscape 6
    The Influence of Online Reviews on Purchasing Decisions 6
    The Psychology Behind Trust and Credibility in Online
    Reviews 7
    The Power of Negative Reviews 9
    The Power of Positive Reviews 9
    The Role of Review Incentives and Manipulation 10
    Conclusion 11

**Chapter 2: Google Reviews: Navigating the Power
of the World's Largest Review Platform** 12
    Introduction: The Rise of Google Reviews 12
    Understanding the Google Reviews Platform 12
    The Importance of Google Reviews for Local Businesses 13
    Leveraging Google Reviews to Enhance Online Reputation
    Management 13
    Tips for Optimizing Businesses' Presence on Google Reviews . 14
    Navigating the Challenges of Google Reviews 15
    The Future of Google Reviews and Online Reputation
    Management 16

**Chapter 3: Facebook: Harnessing the Power of Social
Recommendations** 18
    Introduction: The Evolving Landscape of Online Reviews 18
    Exploring the Role of Facebook in the Review Ecosystem 18
    How Facebook Reviews Differ from Other Platforms 19

The Impact of Social Interactions and Recommendations on Facebook 19

Embracing the Power of Social Recommendations 22

Chapter 4: Yelp: Navigating the Review Landscape for Business Success 23

Introduction: Yelp's Pivotal Role in the Review Ecosystem 23

An In-Depth Analysis of Yelp's Review System 23

The Significance of Yelp for the Restaurant Industry 24

Managing and Responding to Yelp Reviews Effectively 24

Utilizing Yelp's Features to Drive Business Success 25

The Future of Yelp and the Evolving Role of Online Reviews 26

Mastering the Art of Yelp Review Management 26

Chapter 5: TripAdvisor: Navigating the Influential World of Traveler Reviews 28

Introduction: TripAdvisor's Dominance in the Travel Ecosystem 28

The Unique Features of TripAdvisor and Its Impact on the Travel and Hospitality Industry 28

Maximizing Exposure and Reputation on TripAdvisor 29

Strategies for Hotels, Restaurants, and Attractions to Excel on TripAdvisor 30

Hotels: 30

Restaurants: 30

Attractions: 31

The Growing Importance of Traveler Reviews in the Tourism Sector 31

Conclusion: Embracing the Power of TripAdvisor in the Digital Age 32

Chapter 6: G2: Leveraging Peer Reviews in the Software Ecosystem 33

Introduction: The Rise of G2 as a Trusted Software Evaluation Platform 33

Understanding G2's Role in the Software and Technology Industry 33
The Value of Peer Reviews and Ratings on G2 34
How Businesses can Leverage G2 to Showcase their Products or Services 34
Navigating the Software Buying Journey with G2's Insights 35
Embracing the Power of G2 in the Software Ecosystem 36

Chapter 7: Trustpilot: Building Trust through Transparent Customer Feedback 37

Introduction: The Rise of Trustpilot as a Global Trust-Building Platform 37
Examining Trustpilot's Reputation Management Platform 37
Key features of the Trustpilot platform include: 38
The Impact of Trust and Transparency on Consumer Decisions 38
Strategies for Businesses to Build and Maintain a Positive Presence on Trustpilot 39
Harnessing the Power of Customer Feedback to Drive Growth 40
Embracing Trustpilot as a Strategic Trust-Building Platform .. 40

Chapter 8: Angi: Leveraging the Power of Reviews in the Service Industry 42

Introduction: Angi - Bridging the Gap Between Consumers and Service Providers 42
An Overview of Angi's Platform for Connecting Consumers and Service Providers 42
The Role of Reviews in the Service Industry and the Importance of Angi 43
Optimizing Businesses' Profiles on Angi for Maximum Visibility and Credibility 43
Enhancing Customer Experiences Through Angi's Recommendations and Reviews 44
Embracing Angi as a Strategic Partner in the Service Industry 45

Chapter 9: Better Business Bureau (BBB): Navigating the Path to Trust and Credibility 46

Introduction: The Better Business Bureau's Role in Promoting Trust and Consumer Protection 46

Understanding the BBB's Accreditation Process and Its Impact on Businesses 46

Leveraging BBB Ratings and Reviews to Build Credibility and Reputation 47

Strategies for Resolving Customer Complaints and Maintaining a Positive BBB Profile 48

Enhancing Customer Trust and Loyalty Through the BBB 48

Embracing the BBB as a Strategic Partner for Success 49

Chapter 10: Foursquare: Leveraging Location-Based Engagement for Business Growth 50

Introduction: Foursquare's Role in the Service Industry 50

Understanding Foursquare's Location-Based Social Networking Platform 50

Engaging with Customers Through Foursquare's Features 51

Capitalizing on Foursquare's Recommendations and Reviews for Business Growth 52

The Synergistic Benefits of Foursquare Integration 53

Embracing Foursquare as a Strategic Digital Partner 54

Chapter 11: Amazon: Harnessing the Power of Reviews for E-Commerce Success 55

Introduction: Amazon's Dual Role in the E-commerce Landscape 55

The Dual Role of Amazon: E-commerce Marketplace and Review Platform 55

The Impact of Customer Reviews on Product Sales and Reputation 56

Strategies for Sellers to Optimize Their Presence on Amazon Through Reviews 56

Navigating the World of Fake Reviews and Maintaining Authenticity on Amazon 57
The Synergistic Benefits of Leveraging Amazon's Review Ecosystem 58
Embracing Amazon's Review Ecosystem as a Strategic Imperative 59

Chapter 12: RiVirtual: The Power of Virtual Real Estate Reviews 61

Introduction: The Evolving Landscape of Virtual Review Platforms 61
The Rise of Virtual Review Platforms: Transforming the Real Estate Industry.. 61
The Rise of RiVirtual: Revolutionizing the Real Estate Review Landscape 62
Strategies for Businesses to Leverage RiVirtual 62
The Role of Virtual Reviews in Shaping Purchasing Decisions 63
Navigating the Complexities of Virtual Reviews..................... 64
The Future of Virtual Review Platforms in the Real Estate Industry 65
Embracing the Power of Virtual Reviews for Real Estate Success 66

Chapter 13: Harnessing the Power of Goodreviews.co . 68

Understanding the Goodreviews.co Ecosystem 68
The Importance of Goodreviews.co for Your Business 69
Key Benefits of Leveraging Goodreviews.co: 69

Chapter 14: Mastering Reputation Management with Goodreviews.co 75

The Importance of Online Reputation Management 75
Understanding the Goodreviews.co Ecosystem 76
Developing a Comprehensive Reputation Management Strategy... 77

Chapter 15: Next Steps **82**
    Marketing Initiatives to Integrate Goodreviews.co Elements ... 82
    Monitoring and Responding to Negative Reviews 83
    Leveraging Goodreviews.co for Competitive Advantage 84
    The Future of Reputation Management with Goodreviews.co 85
    Key Trends and Developments Shaping the Future : 85
    Enhanced Omnichannel Review Aggregation 86
    Personalized Reputation Management Strategies 86
    Proactive Reputation Monitoring and Predictive Insights 86
    Integration with Other Business Ecosystems 87

Introduction

In the digital age, online reviews have become an integral part of our decision-making process. Whether we are looking for a restaurant, a product, or a service, we turn to platforms like Google Reviews, Facebook, Yelp, TripAdvisor, G2, Trustpilot, Angi, Better Business Bureau (BBB), Foursquare, and Amazon to gather insights from other users. This book aims to provide a comprehensive understanding of these platforms and how they shape our choices in today's interconnected world.

Chapter 1: The Power of Online Reviews
- The significance of online reviews in the modern consumer landscape
- The influence of online reviews on purchasing decisions
- The psychology behind trust and credibility in online reviews

Chapter 2: Google Reviews
- Understanding the Google Reviews platform
- The importance of Google Reviews for local businesses
- Leveraging Google Reviews to enhance online reputation management
- Tips for optimizing businesses' presence on Google Reviews

Chapter 3: Facebook
- Exploring the role of Facebook in the review ecosystem
- How Facebook Reviews differ from other platforms
- The impact of social interactions and recommendations on Facebook

- Strategies for businesses to leverage Facebook Reviews for growth

Chapter 4: Yelp
- An in-depth analysis of Yelp's Review system
- The significance of Yelp for the restaurant industry
- Managing and responding to Yelp Reviews effectively
- Utilizing Yelp's features to drive business success

Chapter 5: TripAdvisor
- The unique features of TripAdvisor and its impact on the travel and hospitality industry
- Maximizing exposure and reputation on TripAdvisor
- Strategies for hotels, restaurants, and attractions to excel on TripAdvisor
- The growing importance of traveler reviews in the tourism sector

Chapter 6: G2
- Understanding G2's role in the software and technology industry
- The value of peer reviews and ratings on G2
- How businesses can leverage G2 to showcase their products or services
- Navigating the software buying journey with G2's insights

Chapter 7: Trustpilot
- Examining Trustpilot's reputation management platform
- The impact of trust and transparency on consumer decisions
- Strategies for businesses to build and maintain a positive presence on Trustpilot
- Harnessing the power of customer feedback to drive growth

Chapter 8: Angi
- An overview of Angi's platform for connecting consumers and service providers
- The role of reviews in the service industry and the importance of Angi
- Optimizing businesses' profiles on Angi for maximum visibility and credibility
- Enhancing customer experiences through Angi's recommendations and reviews

Chapter 9: Better Business Bureau (BBB)
- Understanding BBB's role in promoting trust and consumer protection
- The accreditation process and its impact on businesses
- Leveraging BBB ratings and reviews to build credibility and reputation
- Strategies for resolving customer complaints and maintaining a positive BBB profile

Chapter 10: Foursquare
- Exploring Foursquare's location-based social networking platform
- The significance of Foursquare in the restaurant and hospitality sectors
- Utilizing Foursquare's features to engage with customers and drive foot traffic
- Capitalizing on Foursquare's recommendations and reviews for business growth

Chapter 11: Amazon
- Examining Amazon's role as an e-commerce and review platform

- The impact of customer reviews on product sales and reputation
- Strategies for sellers to optimize their presence on Amazon through reviews
- Navigating the world of fake reviews and maintaining authenticity on Amazon

Chapter 12: RiVirtual

- Exploring the rise of virtual review platforms and their impact
- Understanding the unique features and capabilities of RiVirtual
- Strategies for businesses to leverage RiVirtual to showcase products and services
- The role of virtual reviews in shaping purchasing decisions in the digital age

Chapter 13: Harnessing the Power of Goodreviews.co

- Amplifying your Goodreviews.co presence through integrated marketing
- Monitoring and responding to negative reviews
- Leveraging Goodreviews.co for competitive advantage

Chapter 14: Mastering Reputation Management with Goodreviews.co:

- Developing a comprehensive reputation management strategy
- Optimizing your Goodreviews.co presence
- Integrating reputation into the customer journey

Chapter 15: Next Steps

- Continuous monitoring and refinement

- Building a culture of reputation stewardship
- Expanding Goodreviews.co integration

Online reviews have transformed the way we make decisions in our daily lives. Platforms like Google Reviews, Facebook, Yelp, TripAdvisor, G2, Trustpilot, Angi, BBB, Foursquare, and Amazon have become indispensable sources of information and recommendations. By understanding the dynamics of these platforms and effectively managing online reputation, businesses can thrive in the digital landscape. This book aims to equip readers with the knowledge and strategies to navigate the world of online reviews and leverage them for success in today's interconnected economy.

CHAPTER 1

The Power of Online Reviews

The Significance of Online Reviews in the Modern Consumer Landscape

In the digital age, the influence of online reviews on consumer behavior has become undeniable. As the world becomes increasingly interconnected, individuals from all walks of life have come to rely on the opinions and experiences shared by others online, to guide their decision-making processes. Whether it's a restaurant recommendation, a product review, or a service evaluation, online reviews have become an integral part of the modern consumer landscape.

The rise of platforms like Google Reviews, Yelp, TripAdvisor, and Amazon has transformed the way we gather information and make purchasing decisions. These review platforms have empowered consumers to access a wealth of insights and opinions from their peers, allowing them to make more informed choices and mitigate the risks associated with their purchases. This shift has had a profound impact on businesses, forcing them to adapt their strategies and prioritize their online reputations.

The Influence of Online Reviews on Purchasing Decisions

The power of online reviews lies in their ability to shape consumer behavior and influence purchasing decisions. Studies have shown that the majority of consumers consult online reviews before making a purchase, with some reports indicating that up to 93% of people read reviews before buying a product or service. This trend cuts across various industries, from retail and hospitality to healthcare, and professional services.

One of the primary reasons for this phenomenon is the inherent human desire for social proof and validation. Consumers are naturally inclined to trust the opinions and experiences of others, especially when they can relate to the reviewer's background or preferences. Online reviews provide a platform for these shared experiences, allowing consumers to weigh the pros and cons of a product or service from the perspective of real users.

Moreover, the accessibility and abundance of online reviews have made it easier for consumers to conduct thorough research before committing to a purchase. Rather than relying on limited information from a business's marketing materials or a sales representative, consumers can now access a wealth of unbiased reviews from multiple sources, giving them a more comprehensive understanding of the product or service in question.

The impact of online reviews on purchasing decisions is further amplified by the power of social media and the influence of peer recommendations. Platforms like Facebook and Twitter have enabled the rapid sharing of reviews and recommendations, creating a viral effect that can significantly impact a business's reputation and customer acquisition. Positive word-of-mouth, whether online or offline, can be a powerful driver of sales and customer loyalty.

The Psychology Behind Trust and Credibility in Online Reviews

The credibility and trustworthiness of online reviews are crucial factors that determine their influence on consumer behavior. Consumers are increasingly discerning when it comes to the reviews they trust, and they have developed a keen sense of what constitutes a reliable and authentic review.

One of the key elements that contribute to the credibility of an online review is the perceived authenticity of the reviewer. Consumers are more likely to trust reviews that appear to be written by genuine individuals who have had a direct experience with the product or service, rather than reviews that seem to be written by paid or incentivized individuals. Platforms that prioritize the verification of reviewer identities and the detection of fake or biased reviews have gained the trust of consumers, further enhancing the credibility of the information they provide.

Another important factor in the credibility of online reviews is the consistency and coherence of the reviewer's feedback. Consumers tend to place more trust in reviews that present a balanced and well-reasoned perspective, with both positive and negative aspects of the product or service being addressed. Reviews that appear to be overly one-sided or exaggerated, whether positive or negative, can raise red flags and viewed with skepticism.

The reputation and expertise of the review platform itself also play a significant role in the perceived credibility of the reviews. Consumers are more likely to trust reviews from established and reputable platforms that have a track record of providing reliable information and maintaining high standards of review integrity. Platforms that are transparent about their review policies, have effective measures in place to address fraudulent reviews, and foster a community of engaged and trustworthy reviewers tend to be viewed as more credible sources of information.

Furthermore, the timeliness and relevance of online reviews can also influence their credibility and impact on consumer decision-making. Consumers are more likely to trust reviews that reflect recent experiences, as they exhibit the current state of the product or service. Outdated reviews, or reviews that do not address the specific needs or concerns of the consumer, may be viewed as less relevant and less trustworthy.

The Power of Negative Reviews

While positive reviews can undoubtedly boost a business's reputation and drive sales, the impact of negative reviews should not be underestimated. In fact, research has shown that negative reviews can have a more significant influence on consumer behavior than positive reviews.

Negative reviews can serve as an early warning system for consumers, alerting them of potential issues or problems with a product or service. They are often motivated to seek out and engage with negative reviews to understand the potential risks and drawbacks before making a purchase. This heightened attention to negative reviews can lead to a more thorough evaluation of the product or service, which ultimately benefits the consumer.

Moreover, the way businesses respond to negative reviews can significantly impact the perception of the brand and the credibility of the reviews. Consumers are more likely to trust a business that addresses negative feedback in a professional, empathetic, and proactive manner, demonstrating a genuine commitment to customer satisfaction. Businesses that ignore or dismiss negative reviews, may be perceived as unresponsive and uncaring, which can further damage their reputation.

The Power of Positive Reviews

While negative reviews cannot be ignored, the power of positive reviews should not be overlooked. Positive reviews can serve as powerful social proof, influencing consumers' perceptions of a product or service and their willingness to make a purchase.

Positive reviews highlights the unique features, benefits, and overall satisfaction that customers have experienced. These reviews can help potential customers visualize the value and benefits of the product or service, reducing their perceived risk and increasing their confidence in making a purchase. Businesses that consistently receive positive reviews are more likely to be viewed as trustworthy and reliable, which leads to increased customer loyalty and repeat business.

Furthermore, positive reviews can also have a significant impact on a business's search engine optimization (SEO) and online visibility. Search engines, such as Google, often prioritize websites and listings with a high volume of positive reviews, as they are seen as more relevant and trustworthy to users. This can result in increased organic traffic and improved lead generation for businesses.

The Role of Review Incentives and Manipulation

While the power of online reviews is undeniable, it is crucial to acknowledge the potential review incentives and manipulation that can undermine the credibility of the review ecosystem.

Some businesses have been known to offer incentives, such as discounts or rewards, to customers in exchange for positive reviews. This practice, known as "review manipulation," can skew the overall review landscape and lead to an inaccurate representation of the product or service's true quality and performance.

Similarly, some businesses have been accused of posting fake or biased reviews, either by creating false accounts or by enlisting the help of paid reviewers. This practice, known as "review fraud," can artificially inflate a business's online reputation and lead to misinformed purchasing decisions by the consumers.

To combat these issues, review platforms have implemented various measures to detect and address review manipulation and fraud. These measures include the use of algorithms to identify suspicious review patterns, the verification of reviewer identities, and the implementation of policies that prohibit the use of incentives or the posting of fake reviews.

Businesses too, have a responsibility to maintain the integrity of the review ecosystem by avoiding the use of incentives or other manipulative tactics. Instead, they should focus on consistent delivering of high-quality products and services, and actively encourage genuine customer feedback through transparent and ethical means.

Conclusion

The power of online reviews in the modern consumer landscape cannot be overstated. As they increasingly rely on the experiences and opinions of others to guide their purchasing decisions, the importance of maintaining a positive online reputation has become paramount for businesses across all industries.

By understanding the psychology behind trust and credibility in online reviews, businesses can develop strategies to effectively manage their online presence and leverage the power of positive reviews to drive customer acquisition and loyalty. At the same time, it is crucial to address the challenges posed by review incentives and manipulation, ensuring that the review ecosystem remains a reliable and trustworthy source of information for consumers.

As the digital world continues to evolve, the role of online reviews will only become more prominent. Businesses that recognize the importance of this shift, and adapt their strategies accordingly, will be well-positioned to thrive in the ever-changing landscape of the modern consumer market.

CHAPTER 2

Google Reviews: Navigating the Power of the World's Largest Review Platform

Introduction: The Rise of Google Reviews

In the ever-evolving landscape of online reviews, one platform has emerged as the undisputed heavyweight champion: Google Reviews. As the world's largest search engine, Google has leveraged its dominance to create a powerful review system that has become an essential tool for both consumers and businesses alike.

Understanding the Google Reviews Platform

Google Reviews is a platform that allows users to share their experiences and opinions about a wide range of businesses, products, and services. The platform is seamlessly integrated into Google's search engine, maps, and other services, making it easily accessible to millions of users around the world.

When a user search for a business on Google, the results often include a prominent display of the business's Google Reviews, including the overall rating, the number of reviews, and a selection of individual reviews. This information is not only valuable for the consumer but also crucial for the business itself, as it can significantly impact the business's online reputation and visibility.

The Importance of Google Reviews for Local Businesses

For local businesses, Google Reviews have become particularly crucial. In a world where consumers are increasingly reliant on online information to guide their purchasing decisions, a strong presence on Google Reviews makes a difference between a thriving business and one that struggles to attract new customers.

Local businesses, such as restaurants, retail stores, and service providers, rely heavily on their ability to attract and retain customers from their immediate geographic area. Google Reviews have become a powerful tool in this regard, as they allow customers to share their experiences and provide valuable feedback to potential consumers in the same local market.

By maintaining a positive and responsive presence on Google Reviews, local businesses can showcase their strengths, address any concerns or issues, and build a loyal customer base that is more likely to return and recommend the business to others.

Leveraging Google Reviews to Enhance Online Reputation Management

In the digital age, a business's online reputation is pivotal to its success. Google Reviews play a critical role, as they can significantly impact how a business is perceived by both current and potential customers.

Effectively managing a business's presence on Google Reviews is a key component of a comprehensive online reputation management strategy. By monitoring and responding to reviews, businesses can proactively address any negative feedback, highlight their strengths, and demonstrate their commitment to customer satisfaction.

Moreover, a strong presence on Google Reviews can also positively influence a business's search engine optimization (SEO) efforts. Google's algorithms often prioritize businesses with a high volume of positive reviews, as they are seen as more trustworthy and relevant to the users. This results in increased visibility in search engine, which can translate to more customer inquiries and higher conversion rates.

Tips for Optimizing Businesses' Presence on Google Reviews

To maximize the benefits of Google Reviews, businesses should employ a strategic approach in managing their online presence. Here are some key tips for optimizing a business's presence on Google Reviews:

1. Claim and Verify Your Google Business Profile: Ensure that your business is properly listed on Google and that you have claimed and verified your Google Business Profile. This will allow you to manage your business's information, respond to reviews, and access valuable insights about your customer interactions.
2. Encourage Customer Reviews: Implement a proactive system for asking satisfied customers to leave reviews on Google. This can be done through email, in-person requests, or by including review requests on your website or receipts. Providing a positive customer experience is key to encouraging genuine, positive reviews.
3. Respond to All Reviews: Whether positive or negative, it's essential to respond to all reviews in a timely and professional manner. Positive reviews should be acknowledged and appreciated, while negative reviews should be addressed empathetically and with a commitment to resolving any issues.
4. Monitor and Manage Your Reviews: Regularly monitor your Google Reviews and be proactive in addressing any concerns or issues raised by customers. This may involve addressing specific complaints, clarifying any misunderstandings, or simply acknowledging the customer's feedback.

5. Leverage Review Insights: Analyze the feedback and insights provided by Google Reviews to identify areas for improvement in your business operations, customer service, or product offerings. This can help you better align your strategies with the needs and expectations of your customers.
6. Optimize Your Google Business Profile: Ensure that your Google Business Profile is complete and up-to-date, with accurate and detailed information about your business, products, and services. This can help improve your visibility in Google search results and enhance the user experience for potential customers.
7. Utilize Google Review Badges and Snippets: Incorporate Google review badges and snippets into your website and marketing materials to showcase your positive reviews and ratings. This can help build trust and credibility with potential customers and drive more traffic to your business.

By implementing these strategies, businesses can effectively leverage the power of Google Reviews to enhance their online reputation, attract new customers, and drive long-term growth and success.

Navigating the Challenges of Google Reviews

While the benefits of Google Reviews are numerous, there are also some challenges that businesses must navigate to ensure the integrity and effectiveness of their online presence.

One of the primary challenges is the potential for fake or biased reviews. As with any online review platform, there is a risk of businesses or individuals attempting to manipulate the system through the use of fake accounts or incentivized reviews. This can skew the overall perception of a business and lead to misinformed purchasing decisions by consumers.

To combat this issue, Google has implemented various measures to detect and address review manipulation, including the use of algorithms to identify suspicious review patterns and the verification of reviewer identities. However, businesses must also be proactive in monitoring their reviews and reporting any suspicious activity to Google.

Another challenge is the management of negative reviews. While negative reviews can provide valuable feedback and an opportunity for businesses to address customer concerns, they can also significantly impact a business's online reputation if handled improperly. Businesses must be prepared to respond to negative reviews in a timely and constructive manner, demonstrating their commitment to customer satisfaction and their willingness to address any issues.

Furthermore, the sheer volume of reviews on Google can make it challenging for businesses to stay on top of their review management. As the platform continues to grow, businesses must implement efficient systems and processes to monitor, respond to, and leverage the insights provided by their Google Reviews.

Despite these challenges, the benefits of maintaining a strong presence on Google Reviews far outweigh the potential drawbacks. By embracing the power of this platform and implementing a strategic approach to online reputation management, businesses can unlock a wealth of opportunities to connect with their customers, enhance their brand reputation, and drive long-term growth and success.

The Future of Google Reviews and Online Reputation Management

As the digital landscape continues to evolve, the importance of Google Reviews and online reputation management will only continue to grow. Businesses that recognize the significance of this shift and proactively adapt their strategies will be well-positioned to thrive in the ever-changing world of consumer behavior and decision-making.

The future of Google Reviews is likely to bring even more integration and influence within the broader Google ecosystem, as the search giant continues to prioritize the role of user-generated content and customer feedback in shaping the overall user experience. Businesses must stay attuned to these developments and be prepared to leverage the latest tools and features offered by Google Reviews to maintain a competitive edge.

Ultimately, the success of any business in the digital age will be intrinsically linked to its ability to effectively manage its online reputation. By embracing the power of Google Reviews and implementing a comprehensive strategy for online reputation management, businesses can position themselves for long-term growth, customer loyalty, and market dominance.

CHAPTER 3

Facebook: Harnessing the Power of Social Recommendations

Introduction: The Evolving Landscape of Online Reviews

In the dynamic and ever-evolving world of online reviews, platforms like Google Reviews have dominated the conversation, becoming an integral part of the customer decision-making process. However, as the digital landscape continues to shift, another social media giant has emerged as a powerful player in the review ecosystem: Facebook.

Exploring the Role of Facebook in the Review Ecosystem

Facebook, the world's largest social media platform, has long been a hub for user-generated content, including personal experiences, recommendations, and reviews of businesses, products, and services. While Facebook Reviews may not have the same level of visibility and prominence as Google Reviews, they hold a unique and valuable position within the broader online review landscape.

One of the key advantages of Facebook Reviews lies in the inherent social nature of the platform. Unlike other review platforms that tend to be more transactional in nature, Facebook Reviews are often embedded within the user's existing social network, providing a more personal and trusted source of information for potential customers.

When a user sees a positive review or recommendation from a friend or family member on Facebook, they are more likely to consider that feedback as more reliable and relevant than a review from a stranger on a separate platform. This social validation and the power of personal recommendations can have a profound effect on purchasing decisions and brand loyalty.

How Facebook Reviews Differ from Other Platforms

While Google Reviews and other review platforms focus primarily on the overall quality and performance of a business, Facebook Reviews offer a more nuanced and personalized perspective. Facebook users often share their experiences in a more narrative and conversational style, providing detailed accounts of their interactions, emotions, and impressions.

This level of detail and personal insight can be invaluable for businesses, as it allows them to better understand the specific needs and preferences of their customers. Additionally, the social context of Facebook Reviews can provide valuable insights into how a business is perceived within a particular community or demographic.

Another key difference between Facebook Reviews and other platforms is the potential for ongoing interactions and dialogue. Facebook users can engage with reviews by leaving comments, asking questions, or sharing their own experiences, creating a dynamic and responsive environment that can be leveraged by businesses to build stronger relationships with their customers.

The Impact of Social Interactions and Recommendations on Facebook

The social nature of Facebook Reviews is a significant factor in their impact on consumer behavior. When a user sees a positive review or recommendation from a friend or family member, it carries significant weight than a review from a stranger. This social validation can be a powerful driver of trust and influence, leading to increased engagement, brand loyalty, and ultimately, sales.

Furthermore, the ripple effect of social interactions on Facebook can amplify the reach and impact of reviews. When a user engages with a review by leaving a comment, sharing it, or expressing their approval, that activity is then shared with their own social network, exposing the review to an even wider audience.

This multiplier effect can be a powerful tool for businesses to leverage, as it allows them to tap into the vast social networks of their satisfied customers and turn them into advocates for their brand.

Strategies for Businesses to Leverage Facebook Reviews for Growth

To effectively harness the power of Facebook Reviews, businesses must adopt a strategic and proactive approach. Here are some key strategies for businesses to leverage Facebook Reviews for growth:

1. Claim and Optimize Your Facebook Business Page: Ensure that your business has a well-developed and up-to-date Facebook Business Page, which serves as the central hub for your Facebook presence. Optimize your page with detailed information, high-quality visuals, and a clear call-to-action to encourage customer engagement.
2. Encourage and Respond to Facebook Reviews: Actively, encourage your satisfied customers to leave reviews on your Facebook Business Page. Respond to all reviews—both positive and negative—in a timely and professional manner to demonstrate your commitment to customer satisfaction.
3. Leverage the Power of Social Recommendations: Encourage your satisfied customers to share their experiences and recommendations with their own social networks. Incentivize referrals and word-of-mouth marketing by offering special offers or discounts to customers who share positive reviews.
4. Integrate Facebook Reviews into Your Marketing Strategy: Incorporate your Facebook Reviews into your broader marketing and advertising efforts, using positive reviews and

customer testimonials to build trust, credibility, and brand awareness.

5. Monitor and Analyze Your Facebook Review Insights: Regularly monitor and analyze the feedback and insights provided by your Facebook reviewers to identify areas for improvement, uncover emerging trends, and fine-tune your customer service and product offerings.
6. Engage with Your Customers Through Facebook: Use the interactive nature of Facebook to engage with your customers in real-time, addressing their concerns, answering their questions, and fostering a sense of community around your brand.
7. Collaborate with Influential Facebook Users: Identify and collaborate with influential Facebook users within your target audience, such as industry influencers or brand advocates, to leverage their social influence and reach to amplify the impact of your Facebook Reviews.

By implementing these strategies, businesses can effectively leverage the power of Facebook Reviews to drive customer engagement, build brand loyalty, and ultimately, achieve sustainable growth and success.

The Future of Facebook Reviews and the Evolving Role of Social Media in Online Reputation Management

As the digital landscape continues to evolve, the role of social media platforms like Facebook in the online review ecosystem is only expected to grow in importance. With the increasing integration of e-commerce and social media, the influence of social recommendations and user-generated content is likely to become even more pronounced in the customer decision-making process.

Furthermore, the rise of social media influencers and the growing importance of peer-to-peer recommendations are likely to further amplify the impact of Facebook Reviews on consumer behavior.

Businesses that can effectively navigate this shifting landscape and leverage the power of social media to manage their online reputation will be well-positioned to thrive in the years to come.

Embracing the Power of Social Recommendations

In the dynamic and ever-changing world of online reviews, Facebook has emerged as a powerful player, offering businesses a unique opportunity to leverage the power of social recommendations and personal endorsements to drive customer engagement, build brand loyalty, and achieve sustainable growth.

By understanding the nuances of Facebook Reviews, implementing effective strategies for leveraging this platform, and staying attuned to the evolving trends in online reputation management, businesses can unlock a wealth of opportunities to connect with their customers, enhance their brand image, and position themselves for long-term success in the digital age.

CHAPTER 4

Yelp: Navigating the Review Landscape for Business Success

Introduction: Yelp's Pivotal Role in the Review Ecosystem

In the digital era, where customer reviews hold immense sway over purchasing decisions, Yelp has emerged as a dominant force in the online review landscape. As a platform that specializes in reviews of local businesses, particularly in the restaurant and hospitality industries, Yelp has become an essential resource for both consumers and business owners alike.

An In-Depth Analysis of Yelp's Review System

At the heart of Yelp's success lies its comprehensive review system, which allows users to share their experiences, rate businesses, and provide detailed feedback on various aspects of their interactions. This user-generated content serves as a valuable resource for consumers, helping them make informed decisions about where to dine, shop, or seek services.

One of the key features that sets Yelp apart is its algorithm-driven approach to review curation. Yelp's system employs sophisticated algorithms to identify and highlight the most reliable and informative reviews, filtering out potential fake or biased content. This emphasis on quality and authenticity has helped to establish Yelp as a trusted source of information for consumers.

Furthermore, Yelp's review system goes beyond simple star ratings, allowing users to delve deeper into specific aspects of their experiences, such as food quality, service, ambiance, and value. This level of detail provides business owners with valuable insights into how their offerings are perceived by their customers, enabling them to identify areas for improvement and make informed decisions to enhance the customer experience.

The Significance of Yelp for the Restaurant Industry

The restaurant industry, in particular, has become heavily reliant on Yelp reviews as a critical factor in customer decision-making. Diners often turn to Yelp to research restaurants, read reviews, and make reservations, defining the platform a key driver of foot traffic and sales for restaurants.

A strong Yelp presence can have a significant impact on a restaurant's success, as positive reviews can attract new customers and build a loyal following, while negative reviews can severely damage a restaurant's reputation and deter potential patrons. This heightened importance of Yelp reviews has led many restaurant owners to devote considerable resources to monitoring, managing, and responding to their online reviews.

Managing and Responding to Yelp Reviews Effectively

Effective management of Yelp reviews is crucial for businesses, as both positive and negative feedback can have a profound impact on their success. Business owners must adopt a proactive and strategic approach in managing their Yelp presence, which includes:

1. Regularly Monitoring and Responding to Reviews: Businesses should closely monitor their Yelp page and respond promptly to all reviews, whether positive or negative. This demonstrates a commitment to customer satisfaction and can help mitigate the impact of negative feedback.

2. Addressing Negative Reviews Constructively: When faced with negative reviews, businesses should respond in a professional and empathetic manner, acknowledging the customer's concerns and offering a solution or an opportunity to make amends. This can help to diffuse the situation and showcase the business's dedication to customer service.
3. Encouraging Satisfied Customers to Leave Positive Reviews: Businesses should actively encourage their satisfied customers to leave positive reviews on Yelp, which can help to balance out any negative feedback and showcase the overall quality of the business.
4. Leveraging Yelp's Response Features: Yelp offers the ability to post updates, engage in private messaging, and highlight positive reviews, which can be used to effectively manage the business's online reputation.
5. Analyzing Yelp Data and Insights: Business owners should closely analyze their Yelp data and insights to identify trends, understand customer preferences, and make informed decisions to improve their offerings and customer experience.

Utilizing Yelp's Features to Drive Business Success

Beyond managing reviews, businesses can leverage Yelp's various features to drive their overall success. Some of the key strategies include:

1. Optimizing Yelp Business Listings: Businesses should ensure that their Yelp listings are complete, accurate, and visually appealing, with up-to-date information, high-quality photos, and engaging descriptions.
2. Utilizing Yelp's Advertising and Promotional Tools: Yelp offers a range of advertising and promotional tools, such as Yelp Ads and Yelp Deals, which can help businesses reach new customers, showcase their offerings, and drive sales.

3. Engaging with Yelp's community features: Businesses can actively engage with Yelp's community features, such as responding to reviews, participating in Yelp events, and collaborating with Yelp's elite reviewers, to build stronger relationships with their customers.
4. Integrating Yelp with other digital marketing strategies: Businesses can integrate their Yelp presence with their broader digital marketing strategies, such as website optimization, social media marketing, and email campaigns, to create a cohesive and effective online presence.

The Future of Yelp and the Evolving Role of Online Reviews

As the digital landscape continues to evolve, the role of Yelp and other online review platforms is likely to become even more crucial for businesses, particularly in the restaurant and hospitality industries. With the increasing reliance on mobile devices and the growing importance of user-generated content, businesses that can effectively navigate the Yelp ecosystem and leverage its features to drive customer engagement and business success will be well-positioned to thrive in the years to come.

Mastering the Art of Yelp Review Management

In the dynamic and highly competitive world of online reviews, Yelp has emerged as a dominant force, wielding significant influence over consumer decision-making and the success of local businesses. By understanding the intricacies of Yelp's review system, developing effective strategies for managing and responding to reviews, and leveraging Yelp's features to drive business growth, businesses can position themselves for long-term success in the digital age.

As the importance of online reviews continues to grow, mastering the art of Yelp review management will be a critical component of any comprehensive digital marketing strategy. By embracing this challenge and proactively engaging with their Yelp presence, businesses can unlock a world of opportunities to connect with their customers, enhance their brand reputation, and achieve sustainable growth in the years to come.

CHAPTER 5

TripAdvisor: Navigating the Influential World of Traveler Reviews

Introduction: TripAdvisor's Dominance in the Travel Ecosystem

In the digital age, where travelers have an abundance of information at their fingertips, TripAdvisor has emerged as a leading force in the travel and hospitality industry. As the world's largest travel review platform, TripAdvisor has become an indispensable resource for consumers seeking reliable and detailed information about their travel destinations, accommodations, restaurants, and activities.

The Unique Features of TripAdvisor and Its Impact on the Travel and Hospitality Industry

TripAdvisor's comprehensive review system sets it apart from other travel platforms, offering a wealth of user-generated content that includes ratings, reviews, and detailed insights into various aspects of the travel experience. From hotel amenities and service quality to the ambiance and cuisine of local restaurants, TripAdvisor's review platform provides travelers with a deeper understanding of what to expect, allowing them to make more informed decisions and plan their trips with confidence.

The impact of TripAdvisor on the travel and hospitality industry cannot be overstated. Its influential review system has the power to make or break a business's reputation, as positive reviews can drive increased bookings and revenue, while negative reviews can severely damage the property's establishment's standing, and deter potential customers.

Maximizing Exposure and Reputation on TripAdvisor

Given the significant influence of TripAdvisor, businesses in the travel and hospitality sector must prioritize their presence and reputation on the platform. Effective management of a business's TripAdvisor profile involves several key strategies:

1. Claim and Optimize the Business's TripAdvisor Listing: Businesses should claim their TripAdvisor listing, ensuring that all the information is accurate, up-to-date, and visually appealing. This includes providing detailed descriptions, high-quality photos, and relevant amenities.
2. Actively Monitor and Respond to Reviews: Businesses must closely monitor their TripAdvisor reviews and respond to both positive and negative feedback in a timely and professional manner. This demonstrates a commitment to customer satisfaction and can help mitigate the impact of negative reviews.
3. Encourage Satisfied Customers to Leave Reviews: Businesses should proactively encourage their satisfied customers to leave reviews on TripAdvisor, as this helps to build a strong, positive reputation and balance out any negative feedback.
4. Leverage TripAdvisor's Management Tools and Features: TripAdvisor offers a range of management tools and features, such as Review Express and Business Advantage, which can help businesses effectively monitor, respond, and leverage their online reviews.
5. Integrate TripAdvisor into Broader Marketing Strategies: Businesses can integrate their TripAdvisor presence into their overall digital marketing strategies, including website optimization, social media engagement, and targeted

advertising campaigns, to maximize their visibility and appeal to potential customers.

Strategies for Hotels, Restaurants, and Attractions to Excel on TripAdvisor

While the core principles of TripAdvisor management apply to the travel and hospitality industry, businesses in different sectors may require tailored strategies to excel on the platform:

Hotels:

- Prioritize Guest Experience and Service Quality: Positive guest reviews on TripAdvisor are heavily influenced by factors such as cleanliness, amenities, and staff responsiveness.
- Leverage TripAdvisor's Hotel-Specific Features: Hotels can utilize features like management responses, photo updates, and promotional tools to showcase their offerings and engage with guests.
- Monitor and Respond to Reviews across Multiple Platforms: Hotels should monitor and respond to reviews not only on TripAdvisor, but also on other prominent travel sites to maintain a consistent and positive online reputation.

Restaurants:

- Emphasize Food Quality, Service, and Ambiance: Reviews on TripAdvisor for restaurants often focus on the dining experience, including the quality of the food, service, and overall atmosphere.
- Utilize TripAdvisor's Restaurant-Specific Features: Restaurants can take advantage of features like enhanced listings, menu integration, and reservation management to improve their online presence and customer engagement.
- Encourage Customer Feedback and Respond Promptly: Restaurants should actively solicit feedback from diners and

respond to both positive and negative reviews in a timely and constructive manner.

Attractions:

- Highlight Unique Experiences and Customer Service: Positive reviews for attractions typically emphasize the uniqueness of the experience, as well as the quality of customer service and staff interactions.
- Leverage TripAdvisor's Attraction-Specific Tools: Attractions can use features like virtual tours, photo galleries, and event listings to showcase their offerings and engage with potential visitors.
- Collaborate with TripAdvisor's Community: Attractions can forge partnerships with TripAdvisor's influencers and prominent reviewers to amplify their reach and reputation.

The Growing Importance of Traveler Reviews in the Tourism Sector

As the digital landscape continues to evolve, the role of traveler reviews, particularly those on platforms like TripAdvisor, is becoming increasingly crucial in the tourism sector. Consumers now rely heavily on user-generated content to inform their travel decisions, with TripAdvisor reviews often serving as a primary factor in selecting accommodations, dining options, and activities.

This heightened reliance on traveler reviews has led businesses in the travel and hospitality industry to devote significant resources in managing their online reputation, and leveraging TripAdvisor to drive customer acquisition and loyalty. Businesses that can effectively navigate the TripAdvisor ecosystem and implement strategies to enhance their visibility, ratings, and reviews will be well-positioned to thrive in the highly competitive tourism market.

Conclusion: Embracing the Power of TripAdvisor in the Digital Age

In the dynamic and ever-changing world of travel, TripAdvisor has emerged as a dominant force, wielding significant influence over consumer decision-making and the success of businesses in the tourism sector. By understanding the unique features and impact of TripAdvisor, developing effective strategies for maximizing exposure and reputation on the platform, and tailoring their approaches to the specific needs of hotels, restaurants, and attractions, businesses can position themselves for long-term success in the digital age.

As the importance of traveler reviews continues to grow, mastering the art of TripAdvisor management will be a critical component of any comprehensive digital marketing strategy for businesses in the travel and hospitality industry. By embracing this challenge and proactively engaging with their TripAdvisor presence, businesses can unlock a world of opportunities to connect with their customers, enhance their brand reputation, and achieve sustainable growth in the years to come.

CHAPTER 6

G2: Leveraging Peer Reviews in the Software Ecosystem

Introduction: The Rise of G2 as a Trusted Software Evaluation Platform

In the rapidly evolving software and technology landscape, informed decision-making has become increasingly critical for businesses seeking to invest in the right tools and solutions. Amid the abundance of software options and the ever-changing market dynamics, G2 has emerged as a leading platform that empowers software buyers to make informed decisions through the power of peer reviews and ratings.

Understanding G2's Role in the Software and Technology Industry

G2, formerly known as G2 Crowd, is a renowned software review and ranking platform that has become an indispensable resource for businesses of all size. By aggregating user-generated reviews and ratings, G2 provides a comprehensive and unbiased perspective on a wide range of software products, enabling buyers to make informed purchasing decisions.

The platform's influence extends beyond just software buyers; it also plays a significant role in the overall software and technology ecosystem. Businesses that offer software or technology solutions rely on G2 to showcase their products, connect with potential customers, and build their brand reputation within the industry.

The Value of Peer Reviews and Ratings on G2

At the core of G2's success lies the power of peer reviews and ratings. Unlike traditional marketing materials or vendor-provided information, G2's user-generated content offers a unique, real-world perspective on software products and services. Buyers can access detailed reviews, ratings, and insights from their peers, which helps them better understand the strengths, weaknesses, and overall user experience of the software they are considering.

This user-centric approach to software evaluation has several key benefits:

1. Increased trust and credibility: Peer reviews on G2 are perceived as more trustworthy and reliable than traditional marketing claims, as they provide an unbiased and authentic representation of the software's performance.
2. Informed decision-making: By leveraging G2's data-driven insights, buyers can make more informed decisions that align with their specific business needs and requirements, reducing the risk of costly software investments.
3. Competitive differentiation: G2's review and ranking system allow businesses to distinguish themselves from competitors and highlight the unique features and benefits of their software offerings.

How Businesses can Leverage G2 to Showcase their Products or Services

to Maximize Platform's Benefits, and Businesses in the Software and Technology Industry must Adopt a Strategic Approach:

1. Claim and Optimize the Company's G2 Profile: Businesses should claim their G2 profile, ensuring that all the relevant information, such as company details, product descriptions, and contact information, is accurate and up-to-date.

2. Encourage and Manage Customer Reviews: Businesses should proactively encourage their satisfied customers to leave reviews on G2, while also responding to both positive and negative feedback in a timely and professional manner.
3. Utilize G2's Marketing and Advertising Tools: G2 offers a range of marketing and advertising solutions, including content syndication, targeted advertising, and partnership opportunities, which businesses can leverage to enhance their visibility and reach within the platform.
4. Analyze and Act on G2's Data-Driven Insights: Businesses should regularly review their G2 performance metrics, such as ratings, rankings, and customer feedback, to identify areas for improvement and develop strategies to enhance their software offerings and customer experiences.
5. Integrate G2 into Broader Marketing and Sales Efforts: Businesses can seamlessly integrate their G2 presence into their overall marketing and sales strategies, including website optimization, content marketing, and sales enablement, to create a cohesive and compelling brand narrative.

Navigating the Software Buying Journey with G2's Insights

For software buyers, G2 has become an indispensable resource. From the initial research phase to the final purchase decision, G2's user-generated content and data-driven insights can help buyers navigate the complex software landscape with confidence.

1. Research and Discovery: Buyers can leverage G2's comprehensive database of software products, categorized by industry, use case, and other relevant criteria, to discover and explore potential solutions that align with their needs.
2. Evaluation and Comparison: G2's review and rating system enables buyers to compare software alternatives based on

factors such as ease of use, customer support, and overall satisfaction, helping them make informed decisions.

3. Final Purchase Decision: By considering G2's user-generated insights, including product rankings, user reviews, and customer satisfaction scores, buyers can feel confident in their final software selection and investment.

4. Post-Purchase Validation: Even after the purchase, G2 continue to provide valuable insights, as buyers can monitor ongoing reviews and ratings to ensure that their software investment continues to meet their evolving needs.

Embracing the Power of G2 in the Software Ecosystem

In the dynamic and rapidly evolving software and technology industry, G2 has emerged as a pivotal platform that empowers both software providers and buyers to navigate the complex landscape with confidence. By understanding the value of peer reviews and ratings, businesses can effectively leverage G2 to showcase their products, enhance their brand reputation, and connect with their target customers.

For software buyers, G2 has become an indispensable resource, providing data-driven insights and unbiased perspectives that facilitate informed decision-making throughout the buying journey. As the importance of peer-based evaluation continues to grow, mastering the art of G2 management will be a critical component of any comprehensive digital strategy for businesses in the software and technology sector.

By embracing the power of G2 and proactively engaging with the platform, businesses can unlock a world of opportunities, strengthen their competitive position, and foster long-term success in the ever-evolving software ecosystem.

CHAPTER 7

Trustpilot: Building Trust through Transparent Customer Feedback

Introduction: The Rise of Trustpilot as a Global Trust-Building Platform

In the digital age, where online experiences and reviews hold significant sway over consumer decisions, the importance of trust and transparency has never been greater. Trustpilot, a leading global review platform, has emerged as a critical player in shaping the trust landscape for businesses across various industries.

Examining Trustpilot's Reputation Management Platform

Trustpilot is a customer review platform that allows businesses and consumers to share and engage with feedback about products, services, and experiences. The platform's core mission is to foster trust and transparency by empowering consumers to make informed decisions based on real-world reviews and ratings.

At the heart of Trustpilot's offering is its reputation management platform, which provides businesses with a suite of tools to effectively manage their online presence and cultivate positive customer relationships.

Key features of the Trustpilot platform include:

1. Review Collection and Management: Businesses can invite customers to leave reviews, respond to feedback, and address any issues or concerns raised by customers.
2. Sentiment Analysis and Insights: Trustpilot's advanced analytics provide businesses with valuable insights into customer sentiment, trends, and areas for improvement.
3. Reputation Monitoring and Alerts: Businesses can monitor their online reputation, receive real-time alerts about new reviews, and proactively address any reputational risks.
4. Integration with Other Platforms: Trustpilot seamlessly integrates with a range of popular business and marketing platforms, enabling a streamlined and data-driven approach to reputation management.

The Impact of Trust and Transparency on Consumer Decisions

In the digital age, where information and reviews are readily available, consumer trust has become a critical factor in driving purchasing decisions. Trustpilot's platform plays a pivotal role in shaping this trust landscape, as it provides consumers with a transparent and unbiased view of businesses and their customer experiences.

1. Trust as a Competitive Differentiator: Businesses with a strong Trustpilot presence and positive customer reviews are often perceived as more trustworthy and reliable, giving them a competitive edge in the market.
2. Informed Decision-Making: Consumers can make more informed purchasing decisions by referencing Trustpilot reviews, which provide valuable insights into product and service quality, customer service, and overall satisfaction.

3. Reputation Management and Brand Building: By actively managing their Trustpilot presence, businesses can cultivate a positive brand reputation, address any customer concerns, and demonstrate their commitment to customer satisfaction.

Strategies for Businesses to Build and Maintain a Positive Presence on Trustpilot

To effectively leverage Trustpilot and reap the benefits of trust-building, businesses must adopt a strategic and proactive approach to managing their online reputation. Key strategies include:

1. Claim and Optimize the Company's Trustpilot Profile: Businesses should claim their Trustpilot profile, ensuring that all the relevant information, such as business details, contact information, and brand messaging, is accurate and up-to-date.
2. Encourage and Respond to Customer Reviews: Businesses should actively encourage satisfied customers to leave reviews on Trustpilot, while also addressing any negative feedback in a timely and professional manner.
3. Leverage Trustpilot's Marketing and Promotional Tools: Trustpilot offers a range of marketing solutions, such as review badges, social media integration, and content syndication, which businesses can use to showcase their positive reviews and reinforce their brand's trustworthiness.
4. Monitor and Analyze Trustpilot Performance: Businesses should regularly review their Trustpilot performance metrics, such as review ratings, response times, and customer sentiment, to identify areas for improvement and develop strategies to enhance their online reputation.
5. Integrate Trustpilot into Broader Marketing and Sales Efforts: Businesses can seamlessly integrate their Trustpilot presence into their overall marketing and sales strategies, including website optimization, content marketing, and sales

enablement, to create a cohesive and trust-building brand experience.

Harnessing the Power of Customer Feedback to Drive Growth

Beyond its role in reputation management, Trustpilot's platform can also serve as a valuable source of customer feedback and insights that can drive business growth and improvement.

1. Identifying Customer Pain Points and Areas for Improvement: By analyzing customer reviews, businesses can gain valuable insights into their customers' needs, pain points, and areas where their products or services can be enhanced.
2. Informing Product and Service Development: Businesses can leverage customer feedback from Trustpilot to inform their product roadmap, service offerings, and overall strategic direction, ensuring that they are meeting the evolving needs of their target market.
3. Enhancing Customer Experience and Loyalty: By actively addressing customer concerns and continuously improving based on Trustpilot feedback, businesses can enhance their customer experience, foster brand loyalty, and drive long-term growth.
4. Generating Social Proof and User-Generated Content: Positive Trustpilot reviews can serve as powerful social proof, which businesses can leverage in their marketing and sales efforts to build trust and credibility with potential customers.

Embracing Trustpilot as a Strategic Trust-Building Platform

In the digital era, where trust and transparency are essential for business success, Trustpilot has emerged as a critical platform for companies seeking to build and maintain a positive online reputation. By understanding the impact of customer feedback on consumer decisions and adopting a strategic approach to Trustpilot management, businesses can unlock a wealth of opportunities to enhance their brand reputation, foster customer loyalty, and drive long-term growth.

As the importance of trust and transparency continues to grow in the marketplace, mastering the art of Trustpilot management will be a crucial component of any comprehensive digital strategy for businesses across various industries. By embracing the power of Trustpilot and proactively engaging with the platform, companies can position themselves as trusted and reliable partners, ultimately driving sustainable success in the ever-evolving digital landscape.

CHAPTER 8

Angi: Leveraging the Power of Reviews in the Service Industry

Introduction: Angi - Bridging the Gap Between Consumers and Service Providers

In the digital era, where consumers have high expectations and an abundance of choice, the service industry has been undergoing a profound transformation. Angi, formerly known as Angie's List, has emerged as a leading platform that connects consumers with trusted service providers, revolutionizing the way people find, evaluate, and engage with service professionals.

An Overview of Angi's Platform for Connecting Consumers and Service Providers

Angi is a comprehensive platform that serves as a hub for both consumers and service providers. The platform's core offerings include:

1. Consumer-Facing Services: Angi provides consumers with a searchable database of vetted service providers, comprehensive reviews and ratings, and the ability to request quotes and book appointments directly through the platform.
2. Service Provider Tools and Features: Angi offers a suite of tools and features for service providers, including profile management, lead generation, customer relationship management, and access to a network of trusted consumers.

3. Angi Certified program: Angi's proprietary certification program helps consumers identify top-rated and reliable service providers, providing an additional layer of trust and credibility.

The Role of Reviews in the Service Industry and the Importance of Angi

In the service industry, where personal experiences and word-of-mouth play a significant role in decision-making. Reviews have become a critical factor in shaping consumer trust and behavior. Angi's platform has become instrumental in this landscape, serving as a centralized hub for reviews and ratings of service providers.

1. Informed Decision-Making: Consumers rely on Angi's comprehensive reviews and ratings to research and evaluate service providers, ensuring that they make informed decisions about who to hire for their specific needs.
2. Trust and Credibility: Positive reviews on Angi help service providers build trust and credibility in the eyes of potential customers, differentiating them from their competitors and positioning them as the preferred choice.
3. Reputation Management: Angi's platform enables service providers to actively manage their online reputation, respond to customer feedback, and address any concerns or issues that may arise.

Optimizing Businesses' Profiles on Angi for Maximum Visibility and Credibility

To effectively leverage Angi's platform and capitalize on the power of reviews, service providers must adopt a strategic approach to profile optimization and reputation management. Key strategies include:

1. Claim and Enhance the Business Profile: Service providers should claim their Angi profile, ensuring that all the relevant

information, such as business details, services offered, and contact information, is accurate and up-to-date.
2. Encourage and Respond to Reviews: Businesses should proactively encourage satisfied customers to leave reviews on Angi, while also addressing any negative feedback in a timely and professional manner.
3. Leverage Angi's Certification and Badging Programs: Participation in Angi's certified program and the display of Angi-related badges can significantly enhance a business's credibility and visibility on the platform.
4. Utilize Angi's Marketing and Advertising Tools: Angi offers a range of marketing solutions, such as targeted advertising, content syndication, and lead generation, which businesses can leverage to increase their exposure and attract new customers.
5. Monitor and Analyze Angi Performance: Service providers should regularly review their Angi performance metrics, including review ratings, response times, and customer sentiment, to identify areas for improvement and develop strategies to enhance their online presence.

Enhancing Customer Experiences Through Angi's Recommendations and Reviews

Beyond its role in reputation management, Angi's platform can also serve as a valuable resource for consumers, helping them navigate the service industry and make informed decisions that lead to positive customer experiences.

1. Personalized Recommendations: Angi's algorithm-driven recommendations, based on customer reviews and ratings, help consumers find the most suitable service providers for their specific needs and preferences.
2. Transparency and Accountability: Angi's review system promotes transparency and accountability, as service

providers are incentivized to maintain high-quality customer experiences to maintain their positive ratings and reputation on the platform.
3. Dispute Resolution and Customer Support: Angi's platform offers dispute resolution tools and customer support services, helping consumers address any issues or concerns that may arise during their interactions with service providers.
4. Continuous Improvement: By actively engaging with Angi's review system and customer feedback, service providers can identify areas for improvement, enhance their service offerings, and continuously deliver exceptional customer experiences.

Embracing Angi as a Strategic Partner in the Service Industry

In an increasingly competitive and digitally-driven service industry, Angi has emerged as a critical platform for both consumers and service providers. By understanding the role of reviews in shaping consumer trust and behavior, and by adopting a strategic approach to Angi profile optimization and reputation management, service providers can unlock a wealth of opportunities to enhance their visibility, credibility, and customer relationships.

As the importance of online reviews and recommendations continues to grow in the service industry, mastering the art of Angi management will be a crucial component of any comprehensive digital strategy. Service providers can position themselves as trusted and reliable experts, ultimately driving long-term growth and success in the ever-evolving digital landscape.

CHAPTER 9

Better Business Bureau (BBB): Navigating the Path to Trust and Credibility

Introduction: The Better Business Bureau's Role in Promoting Trust and Consumer Protection

In the complex and ever-evolving world of commerce, the Better Business Bureau (BBB) has long been a trusted name in promoting trust, transparency, and consumer protection. As a non-profit organization that has been in operation for over a century, the BBB has established itself as a respected authority in the business community, serving as a bridge between businesses and their customers.

Understanding the BBB's Accreditation Process and Its Impact on Businesses

At the core of the BBB's mission is its accreditation program, which serves as a seal of approval for businesses that meet the organization's stringent standards. The accreditation process involves a thorough evaluation of a business's practices, including its advertising, customer service, and dispute resolution mechanisms.

1. Eligibility and Requirements: To be eligible for BBB accreditation, businesses must meet a set of standards that demonstrate a commitment to ethical practices, customer service, and transparency.

2. The Accreditation Process: The BBB's accreditation process involves a comprehensive review of a business's operations, including on-site inspections, financial assessments, and a review of the company's history and customer feedback.
3. The Impact of BBB Accreditation: Achieving BBB accreditation can have a significant impact on a business's reputation and credibility. Accredited businesses are granted the right to display the BBB's iconic logo, which serves as a powerful signal of trustworthiness and reliability to potential customers.

Leveraging BBB Ratings and Reviews to Build Credibility and Reputation

The BBB's ratings and reviews system is a crucial component of its role in promoting trust and consumer protection. Businesses that maintain a positive BBB profile can leverage this information to enhance their credibility and reputation in the eyes of both current and potential customers.

1. The BBB's Rating System: The BBB uses a grading scale, ranging from "A+" to "F," to evaluate and rate businesses based on a variety of factors, including customer complaints, business practices, and responsiveness to customer concerns.
2. Utilizing BBB Reviews: Businesses should actively monitor and respond to customer reviews on the BBB's platform, addressing any concerns or issues in a timely and professional manner.
3. Showcasing BBB Accreditation and Ratings: Businesses can prominently display their BBB accreditation and rating on their website, in marketing materials, and in physical locations to signal their commitment to ethical and customer-centric practices.

Strategies for Resolving Customer Complaints and Maintaining a Positive BBB Profile

In the service industry, where customer satisfaction is paramount, effectively managing and resolving customer complaints is crucial for maintaining a positive BBB profile and reputation.

1. Responding to Customer Complaints: Businesses should have a well-defined process for addressing customer complaints, with a focus on timely and empathetic communication, and a genuine commitment to finding a fair and satisfactory resolution.
2. Dispute Resolution Mechanisms: Businesses should leverage the BBB's dispute resolution services, which provide a neutral platform for addressing customer concerns and reaching mutually agreeable outcomes.
3. Continuous Improvement: By analyzing customer feedback and complaints, businesses can identify areas for improvement, implement corrective measures, and demonstrate a commitment to ongoing enhancement of the customer experience.
4. Maintaining a Positive BBB Profile: Businesses should regularly review their BBB profile, monitor their rating and customer reviews, and proactively address any negative feedback or unresolved complaints to maintain a positive and credible reputation on the platform.

Enhancing Customer Trust and Loyalty Through the BBB

By actively engaging with the BBB and leveraging its accreditation, rating, and review systems, businesses in the service industry can significantly enhance their customer trust and loyalty. This, in turn, can lead to a range of benefits, including:

1. Increased Customer Confidence: Businesses with a strong BBB profile and positive reviews are perceived as more trustworthy and reliable, which can translate into higher customer conversion rates and loyalty.
2. Competitive Differentiation: Achieving and maintaining BBB accreditation can help businesses stand out from their competitors, positioning them as industry leaders committed to ethical and customer-centric practices.
3. Reduced Risk of Customer Churn: Effective complaint resolution and a positive BBB profile can help businesses retain existing customers, as they are more likely to continue engaging with service providers they trust and feel valued.
4. Enhanced Online Visibility and Reputation: The BBB's platform and brand recognition can amplify a business's online presence and reputation, making it more easily discoverable by potential customers searching for reliable service providers.

Embracing the BBB as a Strategic Partner for Success

In the service industry, where customer trust and reputation are essential for long-term success, the Better Business Bureau represents a valuable strategic partner. By understanding its role in promoting trust and consumer protection, and by adopting a proactive approach to accreditation, reputation management, and customer complaint resolution, businesses can position themselves as industry leaders, trusted by both current and potential customers.

As the service industry continues to evolve and customer expectations rise, the importance of maintaining a positive and credible BBB profile will only continue to grow. By embracing the BBB as a key component of their overall digital strategy, service providers can unlock a wealth of opportunities to enhance their brand reputation, drive customer loyalty, and ultimately achieve sustained success in the competitive marketplace.

CHAPTER 10

Foursquare: Leveraging Location-Based Engagement for Business Growth

Introduction: Foursquare's Role in the Service Industry

In the ever-evolving digital landscape, the service industry has seen the emergence of innovative platforms that have transformed the way businesses engage with their customers. One such platform that has had a significant impact on the restaurant and hospitality sectors is Foursquare – a location-based social networking app that has become a valuable tool for connecting businesses with their target audience.

Understanding Foursquare's Location-Based Social Networking Platform

Foursquare is a unique platform that combines social networking, location-based services, and user-generated content to create a dynamic ecosystem for businesses and consumers alike.

1. The core features of Foursquare:
    - Check-ins: Users can "check-in" to various locations, allowing them to share their whereabouts with their social network.
    - Tips and Reviews: Users can leave tips and reviews about the businesses they visit, providing valuable insights for other users.

- Recommendations: Foursquare's algorithm curates personalized recommendations for users based on their preferences and check-in history.
2. The significance of Foursquare in the service industry:
    - Foursquare has become a go-to resource for consumers seeking information about local businesses, particularly in the restaurant and hospitality sectors.
    - The platform's location-based data and user-generated content provide valuable insights for businesses to better understand their target audience and optimize their operations.

Engaging with Customers Through Foursquare's Features

To effectively leverage Foursquare for business growth, service providers must embrace the platform's diverse features and integrate them into their overall digital marketing strategy.

1. Claiming and Optimizing Business Listings:
    - Businesses should claim their Foursquare listing and ensure that all relevant information, such as address, hours of operation, and menu items, is accurate and up-to-date.
    - Regularly updating business profiles with new photos, promotions, and other relevant content can help attract and engage with customers.
2. Incentivizing Check-ins and Reviews:
    - Offering special incentives, such as discounts or exclusive offers, for customers who check-in or leave reviews can encourage increased engagement and user-generated content.
    - Responding to reviews, both positive and negative, demonstrates a commitment to customer satisfaction and can help build trust and loyalty.

3. Leveraging Location-based Features:
   - Foursquare's location-based features, such as geofencing and targeted offers, allow businesses to deliver personalized promotions and experiences to customers in proximity to their physical locations.
   - By understanding foot traffic patterns and customer behavior, businesses can optimize their operations and marketing efforts to drive more foot traffic and boost sales.

Capitalizing on Foursquare's Recommendations and Reviews for Business Growth

Foursquare's user-generated content, in the form of reviews and recommendations, can be a powerful asset for service providers looking to enhance their reputation and attract new customers.

1. Analyzing Foursquare Reviews and Insights:
   - Regularly monitoring Foursquare reviews can provide valuable feedback on the customer experience, helping businesses identify areas for improvement and address any concerns.
   - Foursquare's analytics tools offer insights into customer demographics, preferences, and behavior, enabling businesses to make data-driven decisions.
2. Leveraging Foursquare Recommendations:
   - Businesses can leverage Foursquare's personalized recommendations to reach new customers who are likely to be interested in their offerings.
   - By understanding the factors that influence Foursquare's recommendation algorithms, businesses can optimize their profiles and content to increase their visibility and appeal to potential customers.

3. Integrating Foursquare Reviews and Recommendations:
   - Incorporating Foursquare reviews and recommendations into a business's website, social media channels, and other marketing materials can help build trust and credibility with potential customers.
   - By highlighting positive Foursquare reviews and showcasing their Foursquare presence, businesses can differentiate themselves from competitors and attract more foot traffic to their physical locations.

The Synergistic Benefits of Foursquare Integration

By fully embracing Foursquare as a strategic component of their digital marketing efforts, service providers can unlock a range of synergistic benefits that can drive business growth and long-term success.

1. Increased Customer Engagement and Loyalty:
   - Foursquare's location-based features and user-generated content can help businesses foster deeper connections with their customers, leading to improved customer retention and advocacy.
   - Engaging with customers through Foursquare can also lead to the collection of valuable data and insights that can inform future marketing and operational decisions.
2. Enhanced Online Visibility and Reputation:
   - Foursquare's integration with other social media platforms, such as Facebook and Twitter, can amplify a business's online presence, helping them to attract new customers.
   - Positive Foursquare reviews and recommendations can also contribute to a business's overall online reputation, making them more appealing to potential customers in the search for reliable service providers.

3. Competitive Advantage in the Service Industry:
    - By fully leveraging Foursquare's features and capabilities, service providers can differentiate themselves from their competitors and position themselves as industry leaders in customer engagement and digital innovation.
    - Businesses that proactively adopt and optimize their Foursquare presence can gain a competitive edge by anticipating and meeting the evolving needs and expectations of their target audience.

Embracing Foursquare as a Strategic Digital Partner

In the dynamic and ever-changing service industry, integrating location-based social media platforms, such as Foursquare, has become a critical component of a successful digital strategy. By understanding Foursquare's role in the service industry, engaging with customers through its diverse features, and capitalizing on its recommendations and reviews, service providers can unlock a wealth of opportunities to enhance their customer engagement, build brand reputation, and drive sustainable business growth.

As the service industry continues to evolve, leveraging innovative digital tools like Foursquare will only continue to grow. By embracing Foursquare as a strategic partner in their digital marketing efforts, service providers can position themselves for long-term success in the increasingly competitive modern service industry.

CHAPTER 11

Amazon: Harnessing the Power of Reviews for E-Commerce Success

Introduction: Amazon's Dual Role in the E-commerce Landscape

Amazon has firmly established itself as a dominant force in the e-commerce industry, serving not only as a leading online marketplace but also as a powerful review platform that significantly influences consumer purchasing decisions. As businesses and entrepreneurs seek to capitalize on the vast reach and influence of Amazon, understanding the platform's nuances and leveraging its review ecosystem has become a critical aspect of e-commerce success.

The Dual Role of Amazon: E-commerce Marketplace and Review Platform

1. Amazon as an E-commerce Marketplace:
   - Amazon has become one of the largest and most influential online retailers, offering a wide range of products and services to consumers worldwide.
   - For businesses and sellers, the opportunity to reach a vast customer base through Amazon's platform is undeniable, making it a crucial component of many e-commerce strategies.

2. Amazon as a Review Platform:
   - In addition to its role as an e-commerce giant, Amazon is a premier destination for consumers to research, compare, and evaluate products through user-generated reviews.
   - The significance of Amazon reviews cannot be overstated, as they can significantly influence purchasing decisions and shape the reputation of products and sellers on the platform.

The Impact of Customer Reviews on Product Sales and Reputation

Customer reviews on Amazon play a vital role in shaping the success of products and the overall reputation of sellers on the platform.

1. The Influence of Reviews on Consumer Purchasing Decisions:
   - Positive reviews can increase consumer trust, drive product sales, and lead to higher conversion rates.
   - Negative reviews, on the other hand, can deter potential customers and significantly impact a product's sales performance.
2. The Impact of Reviews on Product Reputation and Rankings:
   - Amazon's algorithm considers various factors, including reviews, to determine product rankings and visibility within the platform.
   - Maintaining a high average rating and a large number of positive reviews can improve a product's search rankings and increase its exposure to potential customers.

Strategies for Sellers to Optimize Their Presence on Amazon Through Reviews

To thrive in the competitive e-commerce landscape of Amazon, sellers must implement strategic approaches to effectively manage and leverage the review ecosystem.

1. Proactive Review Generation:
   - Encouraging satisfied customers to leave reviews through post-purchase communication and incentives can help build a robust review profile.
   - Responding promptly and professionally to both positive and negative reviews can demonstrate a commitment to customer satisfaction.
2. Review Monitoring and Management:
   - Continuously monitoring reviews and addressing any concerns or issues raised by customers can help maintain a positive brand reputation.
   - Utilizing Amazon's tools and features, such as the "Amazon Brand Registry," to protect against unauthorized sellers and fake reviews can be a valuable strategy.
3. Review-Driven Product Optimization:
   - Analyzing customer feedback and reviews to identify areas for product improvement can help sellers enhance their offerings and better meet the needs of their target audience.
   - Incorporating customer insights into product development and marketing efforts can lead to increased customer satisfaction and higher sales.

Navigating the World of Fake Reviews and Maintaining Authenticity on Amazon

The prevalence of fake reviews on Amazon poses a significant challenge for sellers seeking to maintain the integrity of their online presence and build trust with consumers.

1. Understanding the Impact of Fake Reviews:
   - Fake reviews, whether positive or negative, can distort the perception of a product's quality and influence consumer purchasing decisions.
   - The presence of fake reviews can erode customer trust and undermine the credibility of a seller's overall review profile.
2. Strategies for Combating Fake Reviews:
   - Leveraging Amazon's review monitoring and removal tools to identify and report suspicious reviews can help maintain the authenticity of a seller's review ecosystem.
   - Encouraging genuine customer reviews through ethical practices, such as post-purchase email campaigns and incentives, can help mitigate the impact of fake reviews.
3. Fostering a Culture of Authenticity:
   - Prioritizing customer satisfaction and delivering high-quality products and services can help build a genuine review profile and establish a trusted brand reputation on Amazon.
   - Engaging with customers transparently and addressing any concerns or issues promptly can further reinforce a seller's commitment to authenticity.

The Synergistic Benefits of Leveraging Amazon's Review Ecosystem

By effectively navigating and leveraging Amazon's review platform, sellers can unlock a range of synergistic benefits that can propel their e-commerce success.

1. Increased Sales and Customer Loyalty:
   - Positive reviews can drive increased product visibility, higher conversion rates, and enhanced customer trust, leading to improved sales performance.

- A strong review profile can also foster customer loyalty, as satisfied customers are more likely to return and repeat purchases.
2. Improved brand reputation and credibility:
    - Maintaining a consistent stream of positive reviews can help establish a seller's brand as a trusted and reliable source, setting them apart from competitors.
    - Leveraging customer feedback to continuously improve products and services can further enhance a seller's reputation and attract new customers.
3. Competitive Advantage in the E-commerce Landscape:
    - Effectively managing the review ecosystem on Amazon can provide sellers with a significant competitive advantage, as they are better equipped to navigate the platform's algorithms and meet the evolving expectations of consumers.
    - By prioritizing review management as a strategic priority, sellers can position themselves as industry leaders and capitalize on the growing importance of user-generated content in the e-commerce landscape.

Embracing Amazon's Review Ecosystem as a Strategic Imperative

In the ever-evolving world of e-commerce, the role of Amazon's review platform has become increasingly crucial for businesses and entrepreneurs seeking success. By understanding the dual nature of Amazon as both a marketplace and a review platform, leveraging strategies to optimize their presence through reviews, and proactively addressing the challenges posed by fake reviews, sellers can unlock a wealth of opportunities to drive sales, enhance brand reputation, and gain a competitive edge.

As the influence of user-generated content continues to grow, the ability to effectively manage and capitalize on Amazon's review ecosystem will be a defining factor in the success of e-commerce businesses. By embracing the review platform as a strategic imperative, sellers can position themselves for long-term growth and establish a strong, authentic presence on one of the most influential e-commerce platforms in the world.

CHAPTER 12

RiVirtual: The Power of Virtual Real Estate Reviews

Introduction: The Evolving Landscape of Virtual Review Platforms

The influence of online reviews has become increasingly pervasive, extending far beyond traditional e-commerce platforms. The emergence of specialized virtual review platforms, such as RiVirtual, has revolutionized the way consumers research and evaluate real estate-related products and services, profoundly impacting the decisions of homebuyers, sellers, and investors.

The Rise of Virtual Review Platforms: Transforming the Real Estate Industry

1. The Proliferation of Virtual Review Platforms:
    - Virtual review platforms have gained significant traction in the real estate industry, providing a centralized hub for consumers to research, compare, and evaluate a wide range of real estate-related services and professionals.
    - These platforms have become essential tools for homebuyers, sellers, and investors seeking to make informed decisions in the complex real estate market.
2. The Unique Features of Virtual Review Platforms:
    - Virtual review platforms exemplified by RiVirtual, offer a range of specialized features that cater to the specific needs of the real estate industry.

- These features often include virtual tours, detailed property listings, and comprehensive reviews of real estate agents, lenders, builders, and other industry professionals.

The Rise of RiVirtual: Revolutionizing the Real Estate Review Landscape

1. Understanding the RiVirtual Platform:
   - RiVirtual is a leading virtual review platform that has emerged as a trusted resource for consumers navigating the real estate industry.
   - The platform provides a comprehensive suite of features, including virtual property tours, detailed listings, and in-depth reviews of real estate professionals and services.
2. The Unique Capabilities of RiVirtual:
   - RiVirtual's advanced technology allows users to experience virtual property tours, providing a immersive and interactive way to evaluate potential homes or investment properties.
   - The platform's robust review system enables consumers to access a wealth of information about real estate agents, lenders, builders, and other industry professionals, empowering them to make informed decisions.

Strategies for Businesses to Leverage RiVirtual

As the real estate industry continues to evolve, businesses that effectively leverage the power of virtual review platforms, such as RiVirtual, can gain a significant competitive advantage.

1. Optimizing Business Presence on RiVirtual:
   - Proactively claiming and managing business listings on RiVirtual to ensure accurate and up-to-date information.

- Actively encouraging satisfied clients to leave reviews, enhancing the overall review profile and building trust with potential customers.
- Responding to both positive and negative reviews in a timely and professional manner, demonstrating a commitment to customer satisfaction.

2. Leveraging Virtual Tours and Multimedia Content:
   - Investing in high-quality virtual property tours and multimedia content to showcase listings, projects, or services in an engaging and immersive way.
   - Utilizing RiVirtual's virtual tour capabilities to provide potential clients with a unique and memorable experience that differentiates the business from competitors.
3. Utilizing RiVirtual's Analytics and Insights:
   - Analyzing the data and insights provided by RiVirtual to gain a deeper understanding of consumer behavior and preferences.
   - Leveraging these insights to refine marketing strategies, optimize service offerings, and better cater to the evolving needs of the target audience.

The Role of Virtual Reviews in Shaping Purchasing Decisions

The impact of virtual reviews on purchasing decisions in the real estate industry cannot be overstated, as they have become an essential tool for consumers navigating the complexities of the market.

1. The Influence of Virtual Reviews on Homebuyer and Investor Decisions:
   - Comprehensive reviews of real estate agents, lenders, and builders on platforms like RiVirtual can significantly

influence the selection process for homebuyers and investors.
- Positive reviews can instill confidence and trust, leading to increased engagement and conversion rates, while negative reviews can deter potential clients from working with a particular professional or service provider.

2. The Importance of Virtual Reviews in the Digital Age:
   - The virtual reviews have become the primary source of information for many consumers researching real estate-related products and services.
   - The ability to access a wealth of user-generated content and insights through virtual review platforms empowers consumers to make more informed and confident decisions.

3. The Synergistic Impact of Virtual Reviews and Virtual Tours:
   - The combination of virtual reviews and virtual property tours on platforms like RiVirtual provides a comprehensive and immersive experience for consumers, allowing them to thoroughly evaluate and compare potential homes or investment properties.
   - This synergistic approach enhances the decision-making process and can lead to higher customer satisfaction and loyalty.

Navigating the Complexities of Virtual Reviews

As the influence of virtual reviews continues to grow, businesses must navigate the complexities of maintaining an authentic and reputable presence on platforms like RiVirtual.

1. Addressing the Challenge of Fake or Biased Reviews:
   - Businesses must be vigilant in monitoring and addressing any instances of fake or biased reviews that may attempt to skew the perception of their services or products.

- Leveraging the reporting and review management tools provided by RiVirtual can help businesses identify and mitigate the impact of any questionable reviews.
2. Fostering a Culture of Transparency and Authenticity:
    - Businesses that prioritize customer satisfaction, deliver high-quality services, and engage with clients in a transparent and responsive manner are more likely to build a genuine and trustworthy review profile.
    - Proactively encouraging satisfied clients to share their experiences can help drown out any potential attempts to undermine the business's reputation.
3. Integrating Virtual Reviews into Overall Marketing and Branding Strategies:
    - Businesses should view virtual reviews as a crucial component of their overall marketing and branding efforts, seamlessly incorporating them into their digital presence and leveraging them to drive engagement and conversion.
    - By aligning virtual review management with broader marketing strategies, businesses can maximize the impact and synergistic benefits of virtual reviews.

The Future of Virtual Review Platforms in the Real Estate Industry

As the real estate industry continues to evolve, the role of virtual review platforms, exemplified by RiVirtual, is poised to become increasingly integral to the decision-making process for consumers.

1. Continued Growth and Expansion of Virtual Review Platforms:
    - The demand for comprehensive, user-generated information and immersive experiences in the real estate

industry is expected to drive the continued growth and expansion of virtual review platforms.
- Businesses that proactively adapt to this trend and leverage the capabilities of these platforms will be well-positioned to thrive in the evolving real estate landscape.

2. The Convergence of Virtual Reviews and Emerging Technologies:
   - As virtual review platforms continue to evolve, the integration of emerging technologies, such as augmented reality and artificial intelligence, may further enhance the user experience and the depth of information available to consumers.
   - This convergence of virtual reviews and cutting-edge technologies could redefine the way consumers research, evaluate, and interact with real estate-related products and services.

3. The Pivotal Role of Virtual Reviews in the Future of Real Estate:
   - Virtual reviews will likely become an increasingly critical factor in the decision-making process for homebuyers, sellers, and investors, as they seek to navigate the complexities of the real estate market with confidence and ease.
   - Businesses that recognize the strategic importance of virtual reviews and proactively leverage the power of platforms like RiVirtual will be poised to thrive in the years to come.

Embracing the Power of Virtual Reviews for Real Estate Success

By understanding the unique features and capabilities of these platforms, businesses can develop and implement effective strategies to optimize their presence, showcase their products and services, and leverage the power of virtual reviews to drive engagement, build trust, and ultimately, achieve long-term growth and success.

As the real estate industry continues to adapt to the changing needs and preferences of consumers, the ability to effectively navigate and capitalize on the virtual review ecosystem will be a defining factor in the success of businesses across the sector. By embracing the strategic importance of virtual reviews, real estate professionals and businesses can position themselves for a prosperous future, catering to the evolving demands of the digital age.

CHAPTER 13

Harnessing the Power of Goodreviews.co

In the ever-evolving landscape of online reviews, one platform has emerged as a powerful tool for businesses looking to attract and retain customers - Goodreviews.co. As a comprehensive review aggregator, Goodreviews.co has become a go-to resource for consumers seeking trustworthy insights on products, services, and experiences across a wide range of industries.

Understanding the Goodreviews.co Ecosystem

Goodreviews.co operates as a centralized hub for reviews from across the web, consolidating feedback from popular sites like Google, Facebook, Yelp, TripAdvisor, and more. By monitoring and analyzing this vast trove of customer data, Goodreviews.co provides businesses with a holistic view of their online reputation and the factors driving consumer behavior.

At the core of Goodreviews.co is its proprietary review scoring system, which algorithmically combines and synthesizes reviews from multiple sources to generate a comprehensive reputation score for each business. This score, ranging from 1 to 100, reflects the overall sentiment and trust level associated with a company, serving as a valuable metric for both businesses and consumers.

Beyond the review scores, Goodreviews.co offers a wealth of additional features and insights to help businesses better understand and engage with their customers. This includes detailed analytics on review volume, sentiment trends, customer demographics, and competitor benchmarking – all accessible through a user-friendly dashboard.

The Importance of Goodreviews.co for Your Business

Having a strong presence on Goodreviews.co can be a game-changer in today's review-driven consumer landscape. As customers increasingly rely on online reviews to inform their purchasing decisions, a positive and well-managed Goodreviews.co profile can be the difference between securing a new customer or losing them to a competitor.

Key Benefits of Leveraging Goodreviews.co:

1. Centralized Reputation Management: Goodreviews.co allows you to monitor and respond to reviews from multiple platforms, including Google, Facebook, Yelp, and TripAdvisor, in a single, streamlined interface. This simplifies your online reputation management efforts, enabling you to stay on top of customer feedback and address any issues or concerns in a timely manner.

2. Reputation Scoring and Insights: The platform's scoring system and detailed analytics provide valuable insights into your business's performance, customer sentiment, and areas for improvement. By understanding your Goodreviews.co score and the factors driving it, you can make more informed decisions to enhance your customer experiences and strengthen your online reputation.

3. Enhanced Visibility and Discoverability: By optimizing your Goodreviews.co profile, you can improve your search engine rankings and make it easier for potential customers to find and learn about your business. Goodreviews.co's prominence in search engine results, combined with its trusted brand recognition, can help you stand out from the competition and attract more qualified leads.

4. Positive Customer Experiences: Proactively engaging with reviews, both positive and negative, on Goodreviews.co can help you address customer concerns, build trust, and foster lasting relationships. Responding empathetically to customer feedback demonstrates your commitment to service excellence and can lead to increased loyalty and repeat business.

5. Competitive Benchmarking: Goodreviews.co enables you to compare your performance against industry peers, allowing you to identify opportunities for differentiation and competitive advantage. By understanding how your business stacks up against the competition in terms of review scores, customer sentiment, and other key metrics, you can make strategic decisions to enhance your market position.

Strategies for Leveraging Goodreviews.co

To capitalize on the power of Goodreviews.co, businesses should implement a comprehensive review management strategy that includes the following key elements:

1. Claim and Optimize Your Goodreviews.co Profile: The first step in leveraging Goodreviews.co is to claim your business's profile on the platform. This allows you to verify your company's information, upload photos and videos, and showcase your unique selling points and positive customer experiences.

When optimizing your Goodreviews.co profile, be sure to:

- Ensure that all business details (name, address, phone, website, etc.) are accurate and up-to-date
- Craft a compelling business description that highlights your products, services, and competitive advantages
- Upload high-quality photos and videos that showcase your business, team, and customer experiences

- Encourage satisfied customers to leave reviews on your Goodreviews.co profile
- Respond promptly and professionally to both positive and negative reviews

By thoroughly optimizing your Goodreviews.co presence, you can create a strong first impression and make it easier for potential customers to learn about and trust your business.

2. Monitor and Respond to Reviews: Regularly monitoring your Goodreviews.co profile for new reviews is essential for maintaining a positive online reputation and addressing any customer concerns in a timely manner. The platform's user-friendly dashboard makes it easy to stay on top of incoming feedback, with real-time notifications and customizable alerts.

When responding to reviews, it's important to strike the right tone. For positive reviews, express genuine gratitude and appreciation for the customer's feedback. For negative reviews, address the issues raised in a calm, empathetic manner, and offer a solution or next steps to resolve the problem. Avoid defensive or confrontational responses, as this can further damage your reputation.

Remember, how you respond to reviews on Goodreviews.co is a direct reflection of your customer service and can have a significant impact on the perceptions of both existing and potential customers. By consistently demonstrating a commitment to addressing customer concerns, you can turn negative experiences into opportunities to build trust and strengthen your relationship with the customer.

3. Encourage Customer Reviews: Actively encouraging your satisfied customers to leave reviews on Goodreviews.co is a crucial component of your review management strategy. The more positive reviews you can generate, the more your business will stand out and be viewed as a trusted, reputable provider in the eyes of potential customers.

There are various strategies you can implement to incentivize customer reviews, such as:

- Email follow-ups after a purchase or service interaction, with a direct call-to-action to leave a review.
- In-store or post-service prompts, such as signage or verbal requests, encouraging customers to share their experiences.
- Review-based loyalty programs that offer rewards or discounts for customers who leave feedback.
- Contextual review requests, such as including a Goodreviews.co link in your email signature or on your website's contact page

When asking customers for reviews, be sure to emphasize the value of their feedback and make the process as seamless as possible. Provide clear instructions on how to leave a review on Goodreviews.co, and consider offering a small incentive (e.g., a discount, gift card) to express your appreciation.

Remember, the key is to strike the right balance between actively soliciting reviews and avoiding the appearance of coercion or manipulation. Maintain a genuine, customer-centric approach, and focus on cultivating authentic, positive feedback that reflects your commitment to excellence.

4. Leverage Review Insights for Continuous Improvement: The true power of Goodreviews.co lies in the wealth of data and insights it provides about your business, your customers, and your industry. By analyzing the feedback and data from your Goodreviews.co profile, you can identify areas for improvement in your products, services, and customer experiences.

Some of the key insights you can glean from Goodreviews.co include:

- Sentiment Analysis: Identify recurring themes, both positive and negative, in customer reviews to understand what's working well and what needs improvement.
- Customer Demographics: Understand the age, gender, and geographic distribution of your customer base to inform targeted marketing and product development efforts.
- Competitor Benchmarking: Compare your review scores, customer sentiment, and other key metrics against industry peers to uncover opportunities for differentiation.
- Operational Insights: Pinpoint specific issues or pain points that customers are experiencing, and use this information to streamline your processes and enhance the customer journey.

By regularly reviewing and acting on the data and insights from Goodreviews.co, you can make data-driven decisions to continually improve your customer experiences and stay ahead of the competition.

5. Integrate Goodreviews.co into Your Marketing and Advertising: Once you've established a strong presence and positive reputation on Goodreviews.co, leverage this asset across your marketing and advertising channels. Highlighting your positive Goodreviews.co ratings, customer testimonials, and review highlights can be a powerful way to build trust, credibility, and brand awareness.

Consider incorporating Goodreviews.co elements into the following marketing initiatives:

- Website: Display your Goodreviews.co score and featured reviews prominently on your homepage and key product/service pages.
- Social media: Share positive customer reviews and testimonials on your social media platforms to boost social proof and engagement.

- Email marketing: Include Goodreviews.co badges, review snippets, and calls-to-action in your email campaigns.

CHAPTER 14

Mastering Reputation Management with Goodreviews.co

A company's online reputation can make or break its success. Customers are increasingly relying on reviews and ratings to inform their purchasing decisions, and a strong, positive reputation can be a powerful competitive advantage. At the forefront of effective reputation management is Goodreviews.co, a comprehensive review aggregator that provides businesses with the tools and insights needed to monitor, enhance, and capitalize on their online presence.

The Importance of Online Reputation Management

In the past, word-of-mouth recommendations from friends and family were the primary driver of consumer behavior. However, the rise of the internet and social media has fundamentally shifted the way people discover, research, and engage with businesses. Today, a single negative online review can have a significant impact on a company's bottom line, as potential customers are quick to form opinions based on the experiences of others.

A strong online reputation not only helps attract new customers, but also fosters loyalty and trust among existing ones. Positive reviews and high ratings on platforms like Goodreviews.co serve as social proof, signaling to consumers that a business is reliable, trustworthy, and worth their investment.

Conversely, a poor online reputation can be detrimental to a company's growth and long-term sustainability. Negative reviews, low ratings, and a lack of engagement can deter potential customers, damage brand credibility, and even lead to a decline in revenue and market share.

This is where the power of Goodreviews.co comes into play. As a centralized hub for managing and enhancing a company's online reputation, Goodreviews.co provides businesses with the tools and strategies needed to take control of their digital footprint and continuously improve the customer experience.

Understanding the Goodreviews.co Ecosystem

At the core of Goodreviews.co is its proprietary review scoring system, which combines and analyzes customer feedback from a wide range of sources, including Google, Facebook, Yelp, TripAdvisor, and more. This comprehensive approach to review aggregation allows businesses to gain a holistic understanding of their online reputation, rather than relying on a single platform's perspective.

The Goodreviews.co score, which ranges from 1 to 100, is a reflection of a business's overall reputation and customer sentiment. This score is then used to provide valuable insights and benchmarking data, enabling companies to identify areas for improvement and measure their performance against industry peers.

Beyond the review scoring, Goodreviews.co offers a suite of features and tools to support effective online reputation management, including:

1. Real-time Review Monitoring and Alerts: Stay up-to-date on new reviews and customer feedback across multiple platforms, with customizable alerts and notifications.
2. Centralized Review Management: Respond to reviews, both positive and negative, from a single, user-friendly

dashboard, streamlining your reputation management efforts.
3. Detailed Analytics and Reporting: Gain in-depth insights into customer sentiment, review trends, and demographic data to make informed, data-driven decisions.
4. Competitive Benchmarking: Compare your business's performance against industry competitors, identifying opportunities for differentiation and improvement.
5. Review Generation and Solicitation: Encourage satisfied customers to leave reviews on Goodreviews.co and other platforms, building a strong foundation of positive feedback.

By leveraging the full capabilities of Goodreviews.co, businesses can proactively monitor, manage, and enhance their online reputation, ultimately driving increased customer trust, loyalty, and revenue growth.

Developing a Comprehensive Reputation Management Strategy

Effective online reputation management is not a one-time exercise, but rather an ongoing process that requires a well-designed strategy and a commitment to continuous improvement. By implementing a holistic approach to reputation management using Goodreviews.co, businesses can position themselves for long-term success in the digital landscape.

1. Claim and Optimize Your Goodreviews.co Profile: The first step in leveraging Goodreviews.co for reputation management is to claim and optimize your business's profile on the platform. This allows you to take control of your online presence, ensuring that all critical business information (name, address, website, etc.) is accurate and up-to-date.

    When optimizing your Goodreviews.co profile, focus on the following key elements:

- Compelling business description: Craft a detailed and engaging description that highlights your unique value proposition, product/service offerings, and competitive advantages.
- High-quality visuals: Upload professional photos and videos that showcase your business, team, and customer experiences.
- Detailed business information: Provide comprehensive details about your company, including operating hours, payment methods, and any relevant certifications or awards.

By taking the time to thoroughly optimize your Goodreviews.co profile, you can create a strong and cohesive online presence that resonates with potential customers and reinforces your brand's credibility.

2. Monitor and Respond to Reviews: Consistent monitoring and timely response to both positive and negative reviews is a critical component of effective online reputation management. Goodreviews.co's user-friendly dashboard makes it easy to stay on top of incoming feedback, with real-time notifications and customizable alerts.

When responding to reviews, it's important to strike the right tone and approach. For positive reviews, express genuine gratitude and appreciation for the customer's feedback. For negative reviews, address the issues raised in a calm, empathetic manner, and offer a solution or next steps to resolve the problem. Avoid defensive or confrontational responses, as this can further damage your reputation.

Remember, how you respond to reviews on Goodreviews.co is a direct reflection of your customer service and can have a significant impact on the perceptions of both existing and potential customers. By consistently demonstrating a commitment to addressing customer concerns, you can turn negative experiences into opportunities to build trust and strengthen your relationship with the customer.

3. Leverage Review Insights for Continuous Improvement
The true power of Goodreviews.co lies in the wealth of data and insights it provides about your business, your customers, and your industry. By analyzing the feedback and data from your Goodreviews.co profile, you can identify areas for improvement in your products, services, and customer experiences.

Some of the key insights you can glean from Goodreviews.co include:

- Sentiment Analysis: Identify recurring themes, both positive and negative, in customer reviews to understand what's working well and what needs improvement.
- Customer Demographics: Understand the age, gender, and geographic distribution of your customer base to inform targeted marketing and product development efforts.
- Competitor Benchmarking: Compare your review scores, customer sentiment, and other key metrics against industry peers to uncover opportunities for differentiation.
- Operational Insights: Pinpoint specific issues or pain points that customers are experiencing, and use this information to streamline your processes and enhance the customer journey.

By regularly reviewing and acting on the data and insights from Goodreviews.co, you can make data-driven decisions to continually improve your customer experiences and stay ahead of the competition.

4. Encourage Customer Reviews: Actively encouraging your satisfied customers to leave reviews on Goodreviews.co is a crucial component of your reputation management strategy. The more positive reviews you can generate, the more your

business will stand out and be viewed as a trusted, reputable provider in the eyes of potential customers.

There are various strategies you can implement to incentivize customer reviews, such as:

- Email follow-ups after a purchase or service interaction, with a direct call-to-action to leave a review
- In-store or post-service prompts, such as signage or verbal requests, encouraging customers to share their experiences
- Review-based loyalty programs that offer rewards or discounts for customers who leave feedback
- Contextual review requests, such as including a Goodreviews.co link in your email signature or on your website's contact page

When asking customers for reviews, be sure to emphasize the value of their feedback and make the process as seamless as possible. Provide clear instructions on how to leave a review on Goodreviews.co, and consider offering a small incentive (e.g., a discount, gift card) to express your appreciation.

Remember, the key is to strike the right balance between actively soliciting reviews and avoiding the appearance of coercion or manipulation. Maintain a genuine, customer-centric approach, and focus on cultivating authentic, positive feedback that reflects your commitment to excellence.

5. Integrate Goodreviews.co into Your Marketing and Advertising

   Once you've established a strong presence and positive reputation on Goodreviews.co, it's time to leverage this asset across your marketing and advertising channels. Highlighting your positive Goodreviews.co ratings, customer testimonials, and review highlights can be a powerful way to build trust, credibility, and brand awareness with potential customers.

Consider incorporating Goodreviews.co elements into the following marketing initiatives:

- Website: Display your Goodreviews.co score and featured reviews prominently on your homepage and key product/service pages.
- Social media: Share positive customer reviews and testimonials on your social media platforms to boost social proof and engagement.
- Email marketing: Include Goodreviews.co badges, review snippets

CHAPTER 15

Next Steps

Amplifying Your Goodreviews.co Presence through Integrated Marketing

Once you've established a strong presence and positive reputation on Goodreviews.co, it's time to leverage this asset across your marketing and advertising channels. Highlighting your positive Goodreviews.co ratings, customer testimonials, and review highlights can be a powerful way to build trust, credibility, and brand awareness with potential customers.

Marketing Initiatives to Integrate Goodreviews.co Elements

Website: Display your Goodreviews.co score and featured reviews prominently on your homepage and key product/service pages. This allows visitors to immediately see your positive online reputation and serves as social proof to support your value proposition.

Social media: Share positive customer reviews and testimonials on your social media platforms to boost social proof and engagement. Encourage your satisfied customers to leave reviews on Goodreviews.co and then showcase these reviews on platforms like Facebook, Instagram, and Twitter.

Email marketing: Include Goodreviews.co badges, review snippets, and links to your profile in your email campaigns. This helps reinforce your reputation and credibility with subscribers, potentially driving them to explore your Goodreviews.co reviews in more detail.

Advertising: Incorporate your Goodreviews.co score, star rating, and review highlights into your paid advertising efforts, whether it's display ads, search engine marketing, or social media advertising. This can be a powerful way to differentiate your business and build trust with potential customers.

Offline collateral: highlight your Goodreviews.co presence in your offline marketing materials as well, such as brochures, flyers, and in-store signage. This creates a cohesive brand experience and reinforces your commitment to customer satisfaction.

By seamlessly integrating your Goodreviews.co reputation into your broader marketing strategy, you can amplify your online presence, attract new customers, and further establish your business as a trusted and reliable provider in your industry.

Monitoring and Responding to Negative Reviews

While the goal of your Goodreviews.co strategy is to cultivate a predominantly positive online reputation, it's inevitable that you will encounter the occasional negative review. These can be challenging to address, but with the right approach, you can turn these situations into opportunities to demonstrate your commitment to customer service and strengthen your relationship with the reviewer.

When responding to negative reviews on Goodreviews.co, keep the following best practices in mind:

Act Quickly: Respond to negative reviews as soon as possible, ideally within 24-48 hours. This shows the reviewer and others that you're actively engaged and committed to resolving their concerns.

Remain **C**alm and **E**mpathetic: Avoid defensive or confrontational language, and instead, approach the situation with empathy and a genuine desire to understand the customer's perspective.

Acknowledge their frustration and express a sincere willingness to make things right.

Offer a Solution: Provide a clear and actionable plan to address the issue, whether it's a refund, a replacement product, or an offer to discuss the problem further. This demonstrates your commitment to customer satisfaction and a willingness to go the extra mile.

Take the Conversation Offline: If the issue requires more detailed discussion or sensitive information, politely invite the reviewer to continue the conversation via email or phone. This helps maintain the privacy and professionalism of the exchange.

Learn from the Experience: Analyze the negative review to identify any underlying issues or areas for improvement within your business. Use this feedback to make targeted changes that can prevent similar problems from occurring in the future.

By consistently applying these best practices when responding to negative reviews on Goodreviews.co, you can mitigate the potential damage to your online reputation and, in some cases, even turn a negative situation into a positive one.

Leveraging Goodreviews.co for Competitive Advantage

By leveraging the insights and tools provided by Goodreviews.co, you can gain a competitive edge and position your business as the preferred choice among your target customers.

Benchmark against Industry Peers: Goodreviews.co's competitive benchmarking capabilities allow you to compare your review scores, customer sentiment, and other key metrics against your industry competitors. This helps you identify areas where you excel, as well as opportunities to improve and differentiate your offerings.

Highlight Unique Value Propositions: Use your positive Goodreviews.co reviews to showcase the unique features, benefits, and customer experiences that set your business apart from the competition. Leverage these testimonials in your marketing and sales efforts to reinforce your value proposition and build trust with potential customers.

Respond to Competitive Threats: Monitor your Goodreviews.co profile for any reviews that mention your competitors, and use this information to inform your strategic decision-making. If you notice a competitor receiving an influx of negative reviews, you can adjust your marketing and customer service efforts to capitalize on their weaknesses and attract those dissatisfied customers to your own business.

Continuously Innovate and Improve: By regularly analyzing the insights from Goodreviews.co, you can identify emerging trends, pain points, and areas of customer dissatisfaction within your industry. Use this information to drive product development, service enhancements, and process improvements that enable you to stay ahead of the competition and exceed customer expectations.

Remember, a strong online reputation is not just a defensive measure – it can be a powerful offensive tool in your competitive strategy. By leveraging the full capabilities of Goodreviews.co, you can proactively shape your market position, attract and retain customers, and establish your business as an industry leader.

The Future of Reputation Management with Goodreviews.co

As the digital landscape continues to evolve, the importance of effective online reputation management will only continue to grow. Goodreviews.co is at the forefront of this transformation, providing businesses with the innovative tools and insights needed to navigate the ever-changing world of customer feedback and review-driven decision making.

Key Trends and Developments Shaping the Future :

Increased Reliance on Artificial Intelligence and Machine Learning: Goodreviews.co is already leveraging algorithms to automate various aspects of the review management process, from sentiment analysis to recommendation generation. As these technologies continue to evolve, businesses will be able to gain even deeper, more actionable insights from their customer feedback, allowing them to make more informed, data-driven decisions.

Enhanced Omnichannel Review Aggregation

While Goodreviews.co currently aggregates reviews from a wide range of sources, the platform's ability to continuously expand its review data collection will be crucial in the years to come. As customers engage with businesses across an ever-growing number of channels, including social media, messaging apps, and emerging review platforms, it will need to adapt to ensure it captures a comprehensive view of a company's online reputation.

Personalized Reputation Management Strategies

As Goodreviews.co's data and analytics capabilities become more sophisticated, the platform will be able to provide businesses with increasingly tailored, industry-specific recommendations and strategies for managing their online reputations. This level of personalization will be essential for helping companies stay ahead of the curve and address their unique reputation management challenges.

Proactive Reputation Monitoring and Predictive Insights

In the future, Goodreviews.co may evolve to offer more proactive reputation monitoring and predictive analytics capabilities. By analyzing real-time data signals and leveraging machine learning algorithms, the platform could potentially identify emerging reputation risks or opportunities before they even manifest, allowing businesses to take preemptive action and stay one step ahead of the competition.

Integration with Other Business Ecosystems

To provide even greater value to its customers, Goodreviews.co may explore deeper integrations with other business software and platforms, such as CRM systems, marketing automation tools, and e-commerce platforms. This would enable businesses to seamlessly incorporate reputation management into their broader operational and strategic decision-making processes.

As the digital landscape continues to transform, Goodreviews.co is positioned to be at the forefront of the reputation management revolution. By continuously innovating and adapting to the changing needs of businesses, the platform will empower companies of all sizes to protect, enhance, and leverage their online reputations for sustainable growth and long-term success.

In today's digitally-driven world, a company's online reputation has become a critical determinant of its success. Customers are increasingly relying on reviews and ratings to guide their purchasing decisions, and a strong, positive reputation can be a powerful competitive advantage.

Goodreviews.co is at the heart of effective online reputation management, providing businesses with the comprehensive tools and insights needed to monitor, enhance, and capitalize on their digital footprint. By claiming and optimizing your Goodreviews.co profile, actively monitoring and responding to reviews, leveraging review insights for continuous improvement, and integrating Goodreviews.co into your broader marketing and advertising efforts, you can build a reputation that truly sets your business apart.

As the future of reputation management continues to evolve, Goodreviews.co is poised to stay at the forefront of this transformation. With its advanced AI and machine learning capabilities, enhanced omnichannel.

www.ingramcontent.com/pod-product-compliance
Lightning Source LLC
LaVergne TN
LVHW041537070526
838199LV00046B/1708